THE INSTITUTE F(

PRESENTS

V O I C E

OF

H E R M E S

~ *Lessons from the Path* ~

MARK STAVISH, M.A.

IHS FOUNDER & DIRECTOR OF STUDIES

∞

ALFRED DESTEFANO III

SERIES EDITOR

Also by Mark Stavish:

- *The Path of Alchemy: Energetic Healing and the World of Natural Magic* (Available in Polish and Russian)

- *Kabbalah for Health and Wellness* (First Edition & Second Revised, Updated Edition; available in Portuguese and Russian)

- *Freemasonry: Rituals, Symbols, and History of the Secret Society* (Available in French, Portuguese, Spanish, and Estonian)

- *Between the Gates: Lucid Dreaming, Astral Projection, and the Body of Light in Western Esotericism* (Available in Portuguese, Russian, and French)

- *The Magical World of Dr. Joseph Lisiewski*

- *Light on the Path: A Study Guide for Qabala, Alchemy & Astrology* (IHS Study Guides, Volume I)

- *The Inner Way: The Power of Prayer and Belief in Spiritual Practice* (IHS Study Guides, Volume II)

- *Child of the Sun: Psychic & Physical Rejuvenation in Alchemy and Qabala* (IHS Study Guides, Volume III)

- *Words of My Teachers: A Companion to the IHS Audio Programs* (IHS Study Guides, Volume IV)

- *Unfolding the Rose: Illumination & Western Esotericism* (IHS Study Guides, Volume V)

- *Mind of Hermes: Visionary Experiences in Western Esotericism* (IHS Study Guides, Volume VI)

- *Pathology of the Sublime: Problems & Solutions on the Spiritual Journey* (IHS Study Guides, Volume VII)

- *Sanctus: The Spirituality of Daily Life* (IHS Study Guides, Volume VIII)

- *The Four Aims: Jupiter in Daily Living* (IHS Study Guides, Volume IX)

- *Pow-Wow: Traditional Folk & Grimoire Magic of the Pennsylvania German Magi* (IHS Study Guides, Volume X)

Continued on the following page...

Contents

Support from the IHS   155

∽ ACKNOWLEDGMENTS ∼

This book is dedicated to everyone on the Path of Return, that they may find peace, wisdom, inspiration, and power in these words. In particular, I express my deepest gratitude to Alfred DeStefano III for his tireless work in bringing these essays to publication. I also restate and reaffirm the support of my wife Andrea Nerozzi and our sons Luke and Nathaniel. Their support these past twenty years has been a source of great strength and inspiration.

∽ INTRODUCTION ∾

The following essays were written over a period of about ten years and discussed a variety of topics that were (at the time) often ignored in spiritual circles: influence of the media, Traditionalism, the notion of the Kali Yuga, and the all-important task of balancing our personal goals with a vision of the bigger picture. Of course, there are also the essays about those individuals who were most influential on my journey, and therefore on my teachings as they are passed on to you. We hope that you not only enjoy these efforts, but find them valuable as guideposts for your own journey on the Path of Return.

THE
BEGINNING
OF THE
PATH

What We Conceive
of Ourselves as Being

19 January 2015

You see, this is the key. All of our successes and failures come down to what we conceive of ourselves as being. In the Gospel, Jesus says, "I and my Father are one."[1] It is written in the Hermetica, "Think of a thing and you are it."[2] Paracelsus states: "If [man] thinks fire, he is fire; if he thinks war, he will cause war."[3] All of the Tibetan Lamas, regardless of them being Bön or Buddhist, Nyingma or of the New School sects, state that the purpose of visualization of the deities—and more importantly of ourselves as the deities—is to awaken ourselves to these qualities that already exist within us. Yes, *they are already within us.* We simply need to recognize them and get out of our own way—get around our false notions and thinking. God tells us, "I am closer to you than the space between your breaths."[4] Jesus says to his disciples, "These things which I do so shall you do and even greater."[5] In the end, it is all about self-image, or more accurately, self-perception.

---

[1] John 10:30.

[2] Cf. *Corpus Hermeticum* XI.19-22.

[3] A. E. Waite (trans.), *The Hermetic and Alchemical Writings of Paracelsus the Great*, Vol. II (London: James Elliott, 1894) 7.

[4] Cf. Alfred, Lord Tennyson: "Closer is He than breathing, and nearer than hands and feet." See "The Higher Pantheism," in *The Works of Alfred Lord Tennyson*, Vol. I (New York: Macmillan, 1908) 602.

[5] John 14:12.

It is a weak self-perception that draws people to magic to begin with. They feel a lack of fulfillment within themselves and believe that there is a secret power in the cosmos that can help them achieve it. To some degree this is true. But instead of having confidence in themselves, they project it out onto something else—their magic wand, the egregore of the order they belong to, their teacher, or the notion of the barbarous words of power in a manuscript of unknown origin. This is the dangerous part, and I paraphrase the librarian and Watcher Rupert Giles who said in an episode of *Buffy the Vampire Slayer*, "All magic is borrowed power."[6]

If we depend upon sigils, signs, and Divine Names to evoke, manifest, and control the forces and intelligences that themselves we conceive of as external to us, then we are damned if there is a mistake or error in the process. The angel will at least have some compassion for us, even if we do not recognize it as such. The demon, however, will have only contempt at our weakness. The rest will show varying degrees of indifference, annoyance, or support, but again, it will be based on their perception of us, which is ultimately based on our own self-image. This is why we perform Assumption of the Godform. As we see ourselves, truly and deeply, so do the host of inhabitants in the invisible.

If the power for that transformation comes from within, then we are invincible. If the power for it comes from without, then we are dependent on it no less than we are on the farmer for our food and the truck driver to deliver it. Just as there is a chain of beings who deliver us our potatoes, so too there is a chain of beings who deliver us our occult powers if we rely on anything outside of ourselves—outside of our own mind and its natural abilities.

When we do offering prayers we are doing them to bring harmony between ourselves and the host of beings that exist in the visible and invisible realms so that they will assist

---

[6]Cf. Season 6, Episode 22: "Grave."

us in our work and be helped by it as well (or at least be indifferent and not hinder us). We may not think of it as such, but consider how many people are involved in a single occult ritual. Think of all of the people needed for you to acquire a simple crystal sphere, or a beeswax candle! At least half-a-dozen, maybe more. But do you ever think of them? The beekeeper, the candle maker, the distributor, the person who fills the order, and maybe another who packs it, or takes it for shipping, and then the people who bring it to your doorstep or to the store where you buy it. How about all of the support people needed to allow each one of these people to do their job? You get the picture. You are not alone in the universe, but you continue to think, feel, and act as if you are, and that others are only there when you need them to do something for you. We call that *selfishness*, and that is the root of all failure. Even criminals must think of the benefits of their criminal acts for all involved. How much less does the average occultist think of their relationship to the vast host of beings in the visible and invisible?

So to assist in this, we perform offerings. This does have a very real effect on our relationships to the "others" we seek meaningful and healthy relationships with, as well as effects on our own psychic body, its psychic centers, channels of force, and the energies that course through them. Each of these centers is not only a gateway, but also a world within us in miniature (a microcosm if you will), wherein these beings exist. This is why the debate about the objective and subjective nature of these beings is infantile and foolish, born out of a lack of experience with the cosmos as it is. These intelligences are both—and our perception and experience depends on our understanding of the forces and intelligences we are dealing with. If you want to consider your experience to be purely subjective and psychological, that is possible, BUT there will be a subtle ripple to the objective equivalent. If you want to consider your experience to be purely objective you may, BUT these forces will still be reflected in your own consciousness, and hence, in the so-called Slingshot Effect Dr. Lisiewski wrote so much about. Your mind is the mirror upon which you experience life—be it a reflection of your high school sweetheart, an angel, a demon, or a saint.

For this reason, you must first learn to understand the nature of your own mind before undertaking communication with non-physical beings. Think of how poorly the average pet owner misunderstands their animal and, as a result, mistreats it. How much more difficult is it to clearly and effectively communicate with beings in another dimension wherein our own mind is the pivot point? To smooth this pathway and to develop a healthy relationship based on mutual respect and understanding of differing needs and values, offerings are essential. Just as you would train your dog or employee through positive reinforcement, so too do you develop your relationships with the inhabitants of the invisible.

The process of offerings is simple, but as with so many things, people may easily fail here. They become either too strict or too lax, rather than understanding the purpose: to create an environment of mutual benefit and, thus, harmony. To this end, we give the best we can, both in terms of physical objects and those visualized. We connect with the inhabitants of the realms through these sense objects as well as our visualizations. How? Through our own psychic centers that correspond to their domains. What we hold back from them, in effect, we are holding back from ourselves. So, like in anything, do your best, give your best, and be kind to yourself and others. Always think of yourself as the giver of "all good things" to all of the realms of creation, and not as a beggar looking for a handout or a conman offering a bribe. No—remember, your self concept is the foundation. You are the enlightened monarch that bestows boons and whom others willingly assist. That is the key to successful offerings, which should be the first step in any ritual act.

Now, in addition, the role of offerings also opens us up to these interior worlds in our dream states, and therefore prepares us for the experience of death. Offerings done simply as a gesture will reverberate negatively on us, so it is not sufficient to think that elaborate rituals offering costly items with intense visualizations are sufficient; they are not if we fail to carry the lesson into daily practice. This entails:

1. Goodwill toward others, but not foolishness.
2. Working to express our best qualities and encouraging others to do so as well.
3. Eliminating the friction of competitiveness by recognizing the cycles of existence and life. Winning and losing are like night and day: both are essential to life as most beings know it.
4. Being content. This is the notion of imperturbability so aptly expressed by Kipling in his poem "If."
5. Treating animals with respect and kindness, particularly those whom you rely upon for your food.
6. Giving alms to those who suffer and experience want.
7. Supporting and providing for spiritual teachings to free people from ignorance, the root cause of all suffering in all of the cosmic realms.

Note that each of these points can easily relate to each of the classes of being and their worlds, as well as to the psychic centers if you so desire. Number One is the mind of the Illumination, the foundation from which we work. Number Two is the realm of the gods or archetypes. Number Three is the angelic realms, the nature of the Archons, the cycles of life itself. Number Four is human existence. Number Five is the animal kingdom. Number Six is the realm of ghosts and the suffering dead. Number Seven is the hell realms and the demonic beings who exist there.

At the end of your offerings give a teaching from your heart to all who are present. This is the basis for many of the practices in the past in soup kitchens and shelters, wherein the attendees would hear a sermon before or during their stay. Even the demons are redeemable, as Christ descended into hell to teach and thereby liberate, or save, the "precarious spirits." Do this and the demons will more readily serve you— if you are worthy—or at the least not obstruct your work or that of others.

If this is done, and we support our rituals and visualizations with genuine acts, then we will neither hope for heaven nor fear hell at the time of death, and will experience the Illumination of our true nature directly and confidently just as it is. We will experience duality and illumination for what they are: states of mind, perceptions, and not concrete realities. The Archons will have been defeated, and Sophia reunited with her bridegroom.

Now that you have the theory, next time we will examine the practice and cover the details of making offerings.

Until then, we leave you once again with the words of Hermes and St. Isaac the Syrian to contemplate.

> 19. Consider this yourself. Command your soul to go anywhere, and it will be there quicker than your command. Bid it to go to the ocean and again it is there at once, not as if it had gone from place to place but was already there. Order it to fly up to heaven and it will need no wings, nor will anything impede it, neither the fire of the sun, nor the ether, nor the whirlwind, nor the other heavenly bodies, but cutting through them all it will soar up to the last body. And if you wish to break through all this and to contemplate what is beyond (if there is anything beyond the cosmos), it is in your power.
>
> 20. See what power you have and what speed! You can do all these things and yet God cannot? Reflect on God in this way as having all within Himself as ideas: the cosmos, Himself, the whole. If you do not make yourself equal to God you cannot understand Him. Like is understood by like. Grow to immeasurable size. Be free from every body, transcend all time. Become eternity and thus you will understand God. Suppose nothing to be impossible for yourself.

Consider yourself immortal and able to understand everything: all arts, sciences and the nature of every living creature. Become higher than all heights and lower than all depths. Sense as one within yourself the entire creation: fire, water, the dry and the moist. Conceive yourself to be in all places at the same time: in the earth, the sea, in heaven; that you are not yet born, that you are within the womb, that you are young, old, dead; that you are beyond death. Conceive all things at once: time, places, actions, qualities and quantities; then you can understand God.

21. But if you lock up your soul in your body, abase it and say: "I understand nothing; I can do nothing; I am afraid of the sea; I cannot reach heaven; I do not know who I was nor who I shall be..." What have you to do with God? For you cannot conceive anything beautiful or good while you are attached to the body and are evil. For the greatest evil is to ignore what belongs to God. To be able to know and to will and to hope is the straight and easy way appropriate to each that will lead to the Supreme Good. When you take this road this Good will meet you everywhere and will be experienced everywhere, even where and when you do not expect it; when awake, asleep, in a ship, on the road, by night, by day, when speaking and when silent, for there is nothing which it is not.

22. Now do you say that God is invisible? Be careful. Who is more manifest than He? He has made all things for this reason: that through them you should see Him. This is the goodness (*to agathon*) of God; this is His excellence: that He is made manifest through all. Though you cannot see what is bodiless, *Nous* is seen in the act of contemplation, God in the act of creation. These things have been made clear to you Hermes thus far. Reflect on all other things in the same way within yourself and you will not be led astray.[7]

---

[7]Salaman, et. al. *The Way of Hermes* (Rochester: Inner Traditions,

What is a merciful heart? It is a heart's burning
for the sake of the entire creation, for men, for birds,
for animals, for demons and for every created thing;
and by the recollection and sight of them the eyes
of a merciful man pour forth abundant tears. From
the strong and vehement mercy which grips his heart
and from this great compassion, his heart is humbled
and he cannot bear to hear or see any injury or slight
sorrow in creation. For this reason he continually
offers up tearful prayer, even for irrational beasts, for
the enemies of truth and for those who harm him,
that they be protected and receive mercy. And in
like manner he even prays for the family of reptiles
because of the great compassion that burns in his
heart without measure in the likeness of God.

God is not One who requites evil, but who sets
evil right. Paradise is the love of God, wherein is the
enjoyment of all blessedness. The person who lives
in love reaps the fruit of life from God, and while
yet in this world, even now breathes the air of the
resurrection.

In love did God bring the world into existence; in
love is God going to bring it to that wondrous trans-
formed state, and in love will the world be swallowed
up in the great mystery of the One who has performed all these things; in love will the whole course
of the governance of creation be finally comprised.

When is a person sure of having arrived at purity?

When that person considers all human beings are
good, and no created thing appears impure or defiled.
Then a person is truly pure in heart.[8]

2004) 57-58.

[8]Wensinck, A. J. (translator), *Mystic Treatises by Isaac of Nineveh:
Translated from Bedjan's Syriac Text with an Introduction and Registers.*
Amsterdam: Uitgave der Koninklijke Akademie van Wetenschappen,
1923. P. 174.

What Did You Come Here For?

9 August 2016

The spiritual path is something that few people come to out of altruism or some desire to know the divine for its own sake—in fact, I will state emphatically that I believe *no one* does. Everyone comes to the spiritual path, the path of understanding themselves, out of a desire to make their lives better. There is something they believe to be (or may actually be) missing—something they seek to acquire though occult means. Now, there is nothing wrong with this, but there is a great deal wrong with not admitting it. The reason is very simple: unexpressed or unrealized desires become toxic. That toxicity can take years or decades to manifest, and its manifestation can occur in the most seemingly harmless of ways.

Well, harmless in *appearance*, anyway.

One of the most common manifestations of this kind of toxicity is when we become overly devoted to "The Work" and, with it, nearly obsessed with the esoteric path and its manifestations—orders, societies, practices—and with seeking to make it an end in itself rather than a *means* to an end. Because that is what these things are: a means to an end. The end, of course, is our original objective when entering the Path. What is it that we were actually seeking to manifest in our life?

You see, it is very easy to get sidetracked on the Path, even dead-ended for quite a while. That sidetracking is mistaken for

11

progress—but progress for who or what? It is very important that we recognize our obligations and debts to those who have gone before us, and provide for those who are here now and who will follow. However, first and foremost we must have something to offer, to be viable role models for others, not just robe-wearing mannequins that move while uttering platitudes or, worse, occult gibberish. We must focus on our "mundane" lives and on expressing our knowledge, wisdom, and compassion in our careers, and not simply wait for the day to end so we can be the esoteric version of Live Action Role Playing (LARPing).

To this end we are once again making available a paper[1] on using esoteric knowledge to achieve your goals and to help you recognize, prioritize, and organize the various areas of your life so that you can achieve what it is you came to esotericism for in the first place.

---

[1] See the following article.

ORDER OUT OF CHAOS

LIFE MAPPING, PLANETARY MAGIC, AND WHY MATTER MATTERS

6 September 2007

I am a child of the earth and of the starry heaven,
but my race is of the heavens...give me cold water
from the Lake of Memory. They will give you water
from the sacred spring and you will live a lord among
heroes.

— "Soul Ladder"[1]

There is a Masonic adage used as the motto of the Scottish
Rite that says, "Order Out of Chaos." While there are a
variety of meanings to this phrase, one in particular is of
importance to us in our daily lives: creating in the tangible
world the life we want.

The key to this, we are told, lies in our subconscious,
in reaching deep into the waters therein and focusing the
power of attraction and concretization it has to bring about
in material form the thing or condition we desire. This is
nothing new to most who are reading this book. Unfortunately, what is new for many is success—regular, reliable,

---

[1]R. C. Hogart, *The Hymns of Orpheus: Mutations* (Grand Rapids,
MI: Phanes Press, 1993).

dependable, predictable success at making things happen and being generally successful in life. To be clear, this is not a success defined by others, but by ourselves—by achieving the goals we set for ourselves, and being happy with the results. This happiness is not a partial happiness born of only partial return, but *total* happiness of a job consciously chosen, undertaken, and completed as we see fit. This is mastery of life; this is mastery of the material world; this is how spiritual consciousness unfolds and gods are born.

This is the sole—or rather the *soul's*—purpose for living in the physical world.

To quote Psellus:

> [Theurgy's] function is to initiate or perfect the human soul [consciousness] by powers of materials here on earth, for the supreme faculty of the soul [consciousness] cannot by its own guidance aspire to the sublimest intuitions, and to the comprehension of divinity.[2]

The Emerald Tablet states: "As above, so below; as below, so above."

And as can be read in the writings of Harvey Spencer Lewis's *Rosicrucian Manual*:

> It may seem strange to the unthinking reader that the study of the law of vibration, with its seemingly endless ramifications, should give us the knowledge whereby we learn to solve economic, social, ethical, and religious problems, yet it does do precisely that. For universal laws are operative in like manner and degree throughout all planes of creation, in all conditions. It may seem stranger yet that by studying the universal and natural laws, as they manifest and apply in the purely material world, mankind should know how they operate in the spiritual world, yet

---

[2]Commentary on the Chaldean Oracles.

such study does just that. By studying about the SEEN world, by recognizing the laws that apply to them, by learning how to make use of those laws that apply to them, by putting them into operation, if altruism is the motive actuating the purpose, the UNSEEN world becomes not only intelligible but as intimately known, contacted, and associated with as the SEEN. By learning how to use natural, universal laws in transmuting material, physical conditions and things, can mankind learn to transmute unfavorable conditions of whatever kind.[3]

Through mastery of the finite we express our infinite mastery.

"Man is God and Son of God, and there is no other God but Man."

To paraphrase Jean Dubuis: *we must learn what we have come here to learn, and take it back with us.*

What we have come here to learn is mastery of matter, of time and space, and through this learning develop or realize awareness of self. This is the work of Becoming, and is expressed in the Egyptian formula "Khepera, Kheper, Kheperu," or, in total, "I became the creator of what came into being. I came into being in the forms of Khepera [Being]. I became the creator of what came into being, that is to say, I produced myself from primeval matter which I made."

We are self-created beings, and our becoming is here, in this world, as only through the mastery of matter and the world of duality can we find our true place in the invisible and experience unity.

In Hermetic practices, symbolism is of prime importance, as it is the manner wherein we begin to communicate ideas to and from our subconscious (and through it the greater collective unconscious mind). Of all possible symbol sets, geometric forms are given the greatest power and importance, as they

---

[3]Harvey Spencer Lewis, *Rosicrucian Manual* (San Jose, CA: AMORC, 1918) 218.

represent both abstract ideas as well as very concrete things (such as crystal formations) and are free of the usual cultural, religious, or superstitious accretions that more specialized symbol sets acquire over time.

In the *Fourth Book of Occult Philosophy*, attributed to Agrippa, we find stated:

> Now we come to speak of the holy and sacred Pentacles and Sigils. Now these pentacles are, as it were, certain holy signes preserving us from evil chances and events, and helping and assisting us to binde, exterminate, and drive away evil spirits, and alluring the good spirits, and reconciling them to us. And these pentacles do consist either of Characters of the good spirits of the superior order, or of pictures of holy letters or revelations, with apt and fit verses, which are composed either of Geometrical figures and holy names of God, according to the course and manner of many of them; or they are compounded of all of them, or very many of them mixt.[4]

The author of the *Fourth Book* further adds: "And if we draw about him any angular figure, according to the manner of his numbers, that also shall be lawful to be done."

This emphasis on geometric shapes and forms is not unique to Medieval and Renaissance European magic but is also found in earlier Middle Eastern practices upon which the former methods drew, as well as in Oriental designs or mandalas. These mandalas, or geometric images designed to present cosmological views in symbolic form, were not limited to paper, stone, or cloth. Tibetan sand paintings, as well as the three-dimensional constructions of the *stupa* (similar in some ways to the old "herms" or road markers of the Classical period), demonstrate the vital importance of

---

[4]Henry Cornelius Agrippa (Stephen Skinner, ed.), *The Fourth Book of Occult Philosophy* (Berwick, ME: Ibis Press, 2005) 34-35.

putting archetypal patterns into material form to allow them to transform and enhance our lives.

Two of the most important geometric forms used to harmonize and integrate the planetary energies that flow across our day are the hexagram and the heptagram.

The Hexagram and Heptagram

The hexagram symbolizes the union of the inner and outer worlds, the harmony of realizing we are beings that can experience physical and spiritual realities without having to choose one above the other, but that both are complementary of the same whole. The upper triangle represents the active life energies of Fire while the lower triangle represents the passive form-creating energies of Water. The symbol is often inscribed with a circle formed out of the serpent Ourobouros (Greek: "tail biter") indicating that the worlds of spirit and matter are both enclosed by the Infinite. The Ourobouros is found in ancient Egyptian temples and may be an expression of the god Mehen. Mehen is the process of gestation before manifestation, and the "protector of the energies" of creation during the formation of the universe. As a chthonic being, it is identified with the invisible energies of the earth and the deepest and most powerful aspects of the unconscious mind. The symbols of the planets are often placed around the points of the triangles according to the flow of energy down the Tree of Life; however, in some alchemical schools, Mercury is placed at the center with the Sun at the top and Mars at the lower-right. In this manner, Mercury represents the union of the worlds through initiation; the Triangle of Fire represents the red metals and the Triangle of Water the white metals.

The heptagram illustrates the flow of energy of the seven ancient planets across the week and day, and represents the harmony of the Seven Planetary Geniuses whose energies vivify and animate life on earth. These also follow the order of the Tree of Life, or the Days of Creation, and are experienced daily with the energies of each individual planet being predominant during one day of the week, even though all are present across the day, thereby assuring a harmonizing of the energies.

For our work we will use the hexagram, as it most completely illustrates the purpose we are working for, while the heptagram complements it in that it demonstrates how the energies we are using work harmoniously throughout our days and weeks through the doctrine of Planetary Hours.

Life Maps and Egyptian Hieroglyphs

The ancient Egyptians often portrayed the lives of important people on the walls of tombs, these being built either prior to or after their birth. The individual's life would be depicted as being victorious in all things, and it was believed that this kind of written affirmation would act as a talisman, thereby creating the desired outcomes for the person for whom it was created. In modern New Age circles we are often told to do something similar, or to map out the life we want. This is to be drawn, illustrated with images or even photographs taken from magazines, thereby allowing us to formulate a literal material representation of what we want to experience in life. For many, this helps organize their thoughts and ideas, where previously there was only disorder. Such maps or collages are orderly and systematic representations of our inner desires made visible for us to see, touch, feel, and emotionally respond to. They help keep us on track when we would stray from our chosen path or become distracted by non-essentials or areas of activity that are none of our concern or that don't support our chosen goals. We quickly learn that if it is not on the map, or has nothing to do with the map, we ignore it.

The Cycles of Cosmic Energy and Our Becoming

Saturn. Real estate, retirement planning, and earthly legacy.

Jupiter. Career, charitable activities, and wealth immediately available for use.

Mars. Physical health and well-being.

Sun. Harmonization of earthly and spiritual functions of self.

Venus. Social and domestic relationships with others; artistic skills and expression of all kinds.

Mercury. Specialized skills and technical knowledge of either a mundane or esoteric nature.

Moon. Subconscious integration, inner personal harmony resulting in psychic skill and the ability to make the subjective objective, and the objective subjective, at will.

All of these relate to the material world; in and through them and their realization we grow personally and as a Being in the universe, and become able to tap into increasingly powerful, abstract, and more cosmological ideas while remaining grounded in the material reality of our choosing, creation, and subsistence. To make use of them, however, we need to have a clear idea, an image with which we can identify and commit our energies for realizing in the material world.

Life Mapping

Make a list of the most important things you need to accomplish under each of the subjects given under the planetary signs. For example, if you are in your forties or fifties and have little money saved, then retirement planning will take precedence over your earthly legacy. If you rent rather than own your own home, real estate may, however, play an important part in your retirement planning, or in how you will fund your children's college education.

After your list is made, even if you have more than one

area of concern for each planet, organize them in order of importance. Pick the most important item from each list and imagine what its accomplished state will be like. What will it feel, look, and be like in all its material form? Find a picture that is either a concrete representation of this desire or that easily, quickly, and without effort evokes the emotions you associate with your desire. For example, if you are saving for your children's education, pictures of graduation caps may be all that is needed, whereas a specific amount of money may be used for retirement planning. If you want a new car but are unconcerned with the make or model, then use an image of a generic car, knowing however what particulars you may want in it (such as good gas mileage, two or four doors, etc.). You can also use a single word to represent each idea as long as you have thoroughly analyzed its meaning and effect on you and are committed to it directing the energies you desire to your intended outcome.

Obtain a large piece of poster board, or better still, a thin, fine piece of wood, and paint on it a large hexagram. Inside each of the vertices of the angles paint the planetary symbol for that point. The ideal is to use colors that are simple, concrete, and easily affect the psyche without effort. A black background with white lines and symbols represents light coming out of darkness, or the individuation of a force or idea, and is a good place to start. Surround the entire image with a circle or, better, a serpent biting its tail.

Starting on a Saturday, preferably in the first planetary hour of the day, place the small pictures, or words, on top of their respective planetary signs. During the week as you meditate on the symbols of the planet of the day, absorb its energy, feel it enter into you, and after several minutes, think of the desired objective you have created for yourself that corresponds to its energy. That is it. Let the energies you have absorbed be linked and directed to your desire by your subconscious in a natural fashion. Allow your imagination to develop the theme, as long as you stay within the boundaries of the theme of the day and do not stray. Now, insights may come to you, showing how each of your objectives relates to the others, and how achieving one will assist in achieving the others. You may even find out that your priorities need to be rearranged. This is fine and is demonstrative of a maturing synthesis within your subconscious taking place.

This subconscious synthesis is the key to all successful magical, occult, or psychic activities, and has been discussed in-depth in *Kabbalah for Health and Wellness*[5] as well as in Joseph Lisiewski's *A Kabbalistic Handbook for the Practicing Magician*[6] and *Hermetic Magic* by Stephen Flowers.[7]

If we are to make full use of our inherent subconscious powers, we must bring them to the level of objective consciousness through careful selection of goals for them, direction of the energy toward those goals, and continued reinforcement of the chosen ideals. Across the day, ask yourself if what you are doing at the moment is positively assisting you in achieving your dreams, or if it is only distracting you. In most instances it is a distraction. Keep your life map where you, and only you, can see it. Talk to NO ONE about it, nor speak of your objectives. Learn to use the power of silence by keeping your thoughts to yourself and hermetically sealing your subconscious from negative suggestions. Know the meaning of the Hermetic axiom of the Sphinx: To Learn, To Will, To Do, to Remain Silent.

Isolation: The Hermetic Womb

The next step on our path of bringing order to the chaotic mass of conflicting emotions, ideas, and instinctual urges that at the moment dominate our subconscious and keep us from

---

[5]Mark Stavish, *Kabbalah for Health and Wellness: Revised & Updated Second Edition* (IHS Publications, 2017).

[6]Joseph C. Lisiewski, Ph.D., *A Kabbalistic Handbook for the Practicing Magician* (Tempe, AZ: New Falcon, 2005).

[7]Stephen Flowers, Ph.D., *Hermetic Magic: The Postmodern Magical Papyrus of Abaris* (York Beach, ME: Weiser, 1995).

fully utilizing its power—a power that turns us into a *cause* in the universe, thereby creating the effects we desire—is cultivating a positive selfishness or healthy ego, a sense of self in the material world, with its relation to others and to the invisible realms.

Dr. Stephen Edred Flowers has noted that there are many similarities between Hermeticism and what is often called the Left-Hand Path (LHP), in his book *Lords of the Left-Hand Path*[8], and in an unpublished appendix to the first edition of his book on the Fraternity of Saturn, *Fire & Ice*,[9] he describes the philosophy and methods of the LHP as follows:

> ...[T]he left-hand path is...the path of non-union with the objective universe. It is the way of isolating consciousness within the subjective universe and, in a state of self-imposed psychic solitude, refining the soul or psyche to ever more perfect levels. The objective universe is then made to harmonize itself with the will of the individual psyche instead of the other way around. Where the right-hand path is theocentric (or certainly allocentric—"other-centered"), the left-hand path is psychecentric, or soul/self-centered. Those within the left-hand path may argue over the nature of this self...but that the individual is the epicenter of the path itself seems undisputed. An eternal separation of the individual intelligence from the objective universe is sought in the left-hand path. This amounts to an immortality of the independent self-consciousness moving with the objective universe and interacting with it at will.[10]

---

[8]Stephen Flowers, Ph.D., *Lords of the Left Hand Path: A History of Spiritual Dissent* (Austin, TX: Runa-Raven Press, 1997).

[9]Stephen Flowers, Ph.D., *Fire & Ice: The History, Structure, and Rituals of Germany's Most Influential Modern Magical Order: The Brotherhood of Saturn* (St. Paul, MN: Llewellyn, 1994).

[10]Cf. Flowers, *Lords of the Left-Hand Path, op. cit.*, 251. Emphasis added].

Given this context it is no surprise that the term "hermetically sealed" refers to a condition wherein nothing can enter from the outside. Using a play on words so typical of Hermeticism (known as "the language of the birds"), we can also read this as being "sealed hermetically," or bearing the seal, mark, or stamp of Hermes, since official seals were the generally accepted means of marking boundaries and warning against intrusion. We need only remind ourselves of the seals on Egyptian tombs used as warnings, or even the use of wax seals on correspondences as a means of keeping their contents private, to understand this symbolism.

Let us compare Flowers's statements to what Dr. Joscelyn Godwin writes in *The Golden Thread: The Ageless Wisdom of the Western Mystery Traditions*:

> A few of the [Chaldean] Oracles suggest that the Juliani [the Roman authors of the Oracles] and their circles also had an idea of bodily transmutation as a means towards immortality. For example:
>
> > The oracles of the Gods declare that through purifying ceremonies, not the soul only, but bodies themselves become worthy of receiving much assistance and health; for say they the mortal vestment of bitter matter will, by this means, be preserved.
>
> ...However, if we try to penetrate this deeper wisdom with the help of modern Hermetic schools, we meet a more esoteric and perhaps disturbing doctrine. According to these schools, while the essence of each human is immortal, it is also impersonal. The personality does not survive, at least not long after the bodily death, and consequently there is nothing left of most people's souls once they have been filtered through the planetary spheres. The vast majority will be extinguished personalities soon after death, while their essence may be recycled as entirely different

entities. To put it plainly, there is no guarantee of
personal immortality, whatever comforting doctrines
may say to the contrary. The ambition of the Hermetic adept is to survive this general dissolution, and
if he should be incarnate again, to do so only through
deliberate choice, not through bondage to a natural
process like everyone else. In order to pass beyond the
boundaries of the cosmos (symbolized by the starry
sphere) and enter consciously into another mode of
existence, the adept must have forged, during his
life, a "radiant body" as vehicle for this individuality.
This is obviously similar to the process described in
the *Chaldean Oracles...* [11]

Further on Godwin quotes Helena Petrovna Blavatsky:

The *permanent* preservation of a personal identity beyond death is a very rare achievement, accomplished
only by those who wrest her secrets from Nature, and
control their own super-material development.... [It
is] accomplished only by adepts and sorcerers—the
one class having acquired the supreme secret knowledge by holy methods, and with benevolent motives,
the other having acquired it by unholy methods, and
for base motives.[12]

Godwin notes that this is possible because the physical
world is not rejected in Hermeticism, but embraced "because
it is infused with celestial influences, is a place of beauty and
wonder." Hermeticism seeks *"useful* knowledge" (like their
later Masonic brethren), and reading and understanding the
Book of Nature is the most useful of all.[13]

---

[11] Joscelyn Godwin, *The Golden Thread: The Ageless Wisdom of the
Western Mystery Traditions* (Wheaton, IL: Quest Books, 2007) 4, 16-17.
   [12] *Ibid.* 17.
   [13] *Ibid.*

Conclusion

If we are to fulfill our Hermetic destiny and function as beings of presence and power in the universe, then mastery of the material world is a good place to start. Let us not be distracted by astral visions and dreams of the gods, but focus on the here and now, and proving to ourselves the efficacy of the doctrines and methods we have chosen. Indeed, the mind—*our* mind—truly is the supreme power in the universe.

Summary

1. The ancients saw the material world as essential to the perfecting of consciousness of the self and the spiritual domain.

2. For laws to be universal they must apply to all conditions at all times, and to the visible world as well as the psychic and spiritual.

3. We can learn about the actions and operations of the psychic and spiritual domains by studying and understanding the material world.

4. The material world is a perfect expression of the subtle ideas of the mind.

5. By mastering matter, we master our mind, our emotions, and ourselves.

6. Mastery is the ability to control, direct, and create the conditions we desire—not, as often stated, denying, repressing, or relegating matter to second-place status.

7. Dualistic philosophies are counter-initiatic, whereas seeing and experiencing the material and spiritual worlds as a single unified expression leads to integration and cosmic Illumination.

8. By consciously organizing and picking those things we want to have in our life, and directing the planetary energies of the day toward them on a regular basis, we harmonize our material, psychic, and spiritual centers of consciousness into a single expression or entity.

9. It is possible to be "self-" or "psyche-" centered without being *selfish* or having disregard for the rights and needs of others.

10. Ancient and modern Hermeticism affirms our "self-created" nature and the absence of a distant creator god. We have created ourselves and created the world in order to evolve our self-awareness.

11. Immortality of consciousness and immortality of the body are seen as the same in several traditional schools.

12. Modern Hermeticism is life-affirming, and sees the material world as good: an expression of divine energy and truth.

Jean Dubuis, Egregores, UFOs, Feng Shui, and Slenderman

5 June 2014

In the 1990s, Jean Dubuis would often lecture about the issue of egregores. For those of you not familiar with the term, John Michael Greer, in *The New Encyclopedia of the Occult*, defines it as "a common term in modern magical practice for the artificial group soul brought into being by...any group of people united by emotional ties of any sort...the gods and goddesses of traditional Paganism are identified as egregores constructed jointly by divine beings and their human worshipers. This corresponds closely to the older Hermetic discussions of the same subject."[1] For Dubuis, far too often the egregore—group mind or soul—was a trap rather than a channel toward liberation. Personal agendas hidden inside the desired manifestations utilized the emotional energy of the group to bring to pass what one person could not—all

---

[1] John Michael Greer, *The New Encyclopedia of the Occult* (Woodbury, MN: Llewellyn, 2003). For further information on the topic of egregores, see the forthcoming book by Mark Stavish, *Egregores: The Occult Entities That Watch Over Human Destiny* (Rochester, VT: Inner Traditions, 2018).

without the knowledge or consent of the group. This was not limited to esoteric or magical circles, but included politics, business, the military, and religious organizations; for this reason, Dubuis advocated a solitary path wherein the external influences could be minimized until they could be effectively managed and made more or less inconsequential.

At the time (around 1994), Dubuis often used the example of a group working in Switzerland whose obsession was with Unidentified Flying Objects, saying that this was all an effort to create a thought form that would materialize so that the group leaders could take on the role of "interplanetary mediators" and thereby gain some significant level of political control that, in his words, "would be worse than Hitler." Having lived through the Nazi Occupation of France (1940-1945), Dubuis speaks here no empty statement nor hyperbole. To this end he would quote his fellow Frenchman, scientist, Rosicrucian, venture capitalist, and author of several bestselling books on UFOs, Jacques Vallée. Vallée is famous for being the inspiration and technical force behind the Steven Spielberg movie *Close Encounters of the Third Kind*.

Vallée is renowned for his scientific investigation of UFO phenomena, and having started his research looking for an extra-terrestrial source for UFOs, ultimately came to the conclusion that these were inter-dimensional beings. His research is detailed in his third book, *Passport to Magonia: From Folklore to Flying Saucers*.[2] He also advocated that UFO phenomena was multifaceted, and included manipulation by government and non-government entities of the sightings, whether they are real, false, or fabricated to manipulate people into believing in the benevolent "space brothers," as some cults have called them. These entities (like the "Unknown Superiors") always seemed to speak through their "chosen representatives" and foretell certain doom that would befall humanity, resulting in mass death—save for the "elect." This

---

[2]Jacques Vallée, *Passport to Magonia: From Folklore to Flying Saucers* (Chicago: Regnery, 1969).

message did not resonate well with Vallée. Maybe the "space brothers" and their self-appointed representatives were not so benevolent after all.

Dubuis also stated that he had been contacted by a magical group in the Channel Islands who invited him to work with them in their efforts to destroy (or at least weaken) the egregore of Islam—this was five years before the "September 11" terrorist attacks and the launching of the "War on Terror." He declined the offer, stating that he had other work to focus on.

What does this have to do with Slenderman, the fictional character who is said to abduct children and be a new source of horror in the world? Everything, really. Using the magical method of the egregore, "What I cannot do alone, many others can do for me." *Read that again.* You see, harnessing the psycho-sexual-emotional energy of millions of pre-adolescent and adolescent youths provides a veritable buffet of psychic energy. To think that you can give them something to focus it on and that it will *not* come into being in some form is either the statement of a fool or a liar.

Let quote the words of Dr. Baolin Wu from his work (with Jessica Eckstein) *Lighting the Eye of the Dragon: Inner Secrets of Taoist Feng Shui*:

> In 1966, shortly before the beginning of the Cultural Revolution, Dr. Wu's teacher, Master Du, took him aside to tell him that China was soon going to be in the throes of revolution. Dr. Wu asked his teacher how could he know such a thing. His response was, "It's part of the *I Ching*. You can predict things." Master Du asked his student what he had seen that morning on his way to school. The young Dr. Wu said there had been a group of children playing with a top, a common toy on the streets of Beijing, whipping it with a string to keep it spinning. Master Du explained that the way they whipped the top was like the way of whipping people, the capturing of people, this was a

sign. It is the will of heaven to warn us ahead of time about everything that will happen, whether we realize it or not. The study of Feng Shui and of the *I Ching* is an attempt to recognize these messages ahead of time... Respecting children as representatives of our collective unconscious is a valuable lesson to learn. ...Whatever a child plays at or with will be what the nation builds up or develops."[3]

The last line is the real lesson here. In closing, let me again quote *Lighting the Eye of the Dragon*, with the question that follows the above statement, "How do you put this concept to use?"[4]

So, how do you?

The Power of the Egregore...Watch Your Dreams

28 October 2015

I often write about those wonderful collective entities known as *egregores*.[5] These guardians of the various traditions are a mixed blessing, as many have discovered, particularly those who have spoken to me privately to help resolve their various spiritual crises as they relate to mystical and magical affiliations and orders—and their separation from them in particular. However, the power of an egregore is also an ambient entity, simply radiating its influence in a given geographic area. Just as we feed, so does it feed. Just as we inhale and exhale, so does it inhale and exhale. The following is from emails I received from a patron and student, and I am sure that it will be of interest to everyone reading this book.

---

[3] Chapter 3, "Sensing the Qi," in Dr. Baolin Wu and Jessica Eckstein, *Lighting the Eye of the Dragon: Inner Secrets of Taoist Feng Shui* (New York: St. Martin's Press, 2000).

[4] *Ibid.*

[5] See the forthcoming book on this topic by Mark Stavish, *op. cit.*

On Sunday, after both I and my wife woke early at 4:30 AM because of a restless sleep and her having a headache, we were finally able to catch some rest a few hours later. During this period I had the following dream. An older Tibetan Buddhist monk gave a long teaching. He went on in a language I did not understand, but there was a translation in my mind. Later in the day during meditation, I "found" him again, and asked him his name, and he replied, "Lama Shugden." Today I was informed by two of my clients that the dharma center five miles from my office gave a Dorje Shugden empowerment yesterday, the morning of my dream experience.

Now, Dorje Shugden is a very suspect practice, even among the Gelukpa for whom it was a main practice starting sometime in the late-nineteenth century. This practice also involves what I attempted to discuss in a series of Facebook posts some time ago, about sacrifice and spiritual imprisonment. While too long to discuss here, you may want to look into the extreme controversy of this Gelukpa Protector practice, and why the Dali Lama has distanced himself from it, and discourages it. Again, in Western terms, it is the power of the egregore and those who benefit from it.

I recently had the opportunity to see the much-vaunted new Batman movie, *The Dark Knight*. For those of you who have not seen it, well, it lives up to the hype. It is well written, directed, acted, shot, and edited—not to mention *long*. However, in one respect, despite all of this, should you not see it, well, then you can still die happy. Without giving away any spoilers, the story is in many ways a concrete reflection of some of the deepest yearnings in the American— and I must say, the collective—consciousness of the world.

This is in part because the United States of America, being born under the sign of Cancer is, generally speaking, a nation of deep reflection (despite appearances to the contrary). It is also moved by inner yearnings and unconscious impulses that sweep into manifestation. Like movies, television, and the entertainment industry, we have come to believe and accept that, for the most part, America is the "land of opportunity" or where the dreams of the psyche can come true. However, along with dreams of health, happiness, progress, and spiritual awakening, there are also shadow figures, demons, and a host of anti-dreams—nightmares that are secretly and even publicly cultivated by individuals and groups, whose primary tool is the mass media.

Given that America exports the majority of films and

radio shows that it produces to the rest of the world, their content plays a significant role in becoming the stuff that fills and shapes the collective consciousness of the world we live in. I find it no surprise that there should be a news story this week of a man being murdered and decapitated as he slept on a Greyhound Bus trip, the murderer subsequently carrying the victim's head to the front of the bus to taunt those who watched in horror outside. Is there a connection between this and the millions of minds watching mayhem unfold in Gotham City? Of course there is. There is only one mind, and what we put into it shapes our collective reality.

For us, that means *The Dark Knight* is more than just a metaphor for the unlikely hero; it is also a stage of psychic breakdown and reduction, wherein each of us is forced to address what really matters, to separate what is true from what is false. The hero who seeks to do the right thing for the wrong reasons (in the case of Bruce Wayne as Batman, revenge for the murder of his parents when he was a child) meets the villain who does the wrong thing for the right reasons (the Joker, who brings anarchy into the world to show that people are for the most part constrained by self-imposed rules, even Batman). This meeting of two opposites means that the average person who tries to do the right thing for the right reasons are caught in the middle of a fight in which they have little power of influence as long as they keep playing by the rules of conventional morality and ethics.

In some respects, we can see Bruce Wayne/Batman as a tantric adept or Magus, capable of wielding tremendous power, shaping the world as he wills, and doing so behind the mask of Dianic Darkness. He has limits, but acts as if he has none. He has total confidence, focus, and is victorious in that he allows nothing to deter him from his chosen goal, and pays whatever price it asks. He, as the Tibetan Buddhists say, brings his anger and rage into the path and uses them for something beneficial even at a cost to himself. Batman is the Wrathful Deity that knows its actions are right because they are right for the particular moment in which they are done, and not for another. He is the gargoyle that sits like a guardian above Gotham City, looking to frighten the wrongdoers, but it is too late. The enemy is not at the gates—it has already entered the city.

In *The Dark Knight,* we also see a more disturbing reflection of our collective psyche, in that ever since Charles Manson appeared on the scene, the various media have begun to portray evil as "sexy." This trend reached its full expression with Hannibal "The Cannibal" Lecter, M.D., who was not only sadistic and vicious, but also a genius. Raw attraction to such a character being so out of touch with reality is testimony to its underlying danger. Wherein like the guards of the infamous death camps of Nazi Germany or Khmer Rouge's killing fields, serial killers to date have shown themselves in reality to be below average in intelligence, under-performers with nothing special about themselves; they are distinguished only by the number of human beings they have murdered. With the Joker, we see evil taken to the next level, nearly supernatural in that he is a veritable incarnation, a force rather than an individual.

On one level, with Batman we see good taken to the extreme, an extreme out of touch with earlier expressions of good as an individual expression within the collective integrity of society. It is no surprise that after two generations of castrating the Western male and advocating for the "mommy state" of cradle-to-grave safety from ourselves as well as every possible imagined danger, the hero *du jour* in a collapsing metrosexual, self-indulgent, media-zombied culture would be a man of pure force—pure in that it is single-focused; pure because it acts knowing what is right and what needs to be done without asking for mommy's permission, and yet must wear a mask to protect its true identity, because the very sheep he seeks to save will suddenly become the hyenas that scavenge for his wounded bones given the opportunity. Batman is the cry for a savior, another messianic mythology for the twenty-first century.

Maybe we should look to the legendary poet Tagore for inspiration, where we read,

> Let me not pray to be sheltered from dangers
> but to be fearless facing them.
> Let me not beg for stilling of my pain
> but for the heart to conquer it.
> Let me not look for allies in life's battlefield
> but to my own strength.
> Let me not crave in anxious fear to be saved
> but for hope and patience to win my freedom.

How does this relate to 2012, you ask? Very simple. What will good people do when the world is broken? When the system no longer works? When corruption is everywhere and no one can be trusted? This is the secondary theme of *The Dark Knight*, and each one of us will be forced to answer it at some point in our lives, be it on some grand scale or in the smaller microcosm of our church, neighborhood, or borough politics.

To quote Count Keyserling, "Man is exactly as immortal as his ideal and exactly as real as the energy with which he serves it."[1] *The Dark Knight* has made over $324 million in eleven days of release, not including the money spent on refreshments, gas, parking, or toys and collectibles made by China, Inc. Given the amount of energy put into *The Dark Knight* and its sadomasochistic themes of alienation, chaos, fear, and hypocrisy, it is time that we rethink our individual and collective ideals.

---

[1] Quoted in Lama Anagarika Govinda, *Foundations of Tibetan Mysticism* (York Beach, ME: Red Wheel/Weiser, 1969) 277.

HERMETICISM
AND THE
PATH OF AWAKENING

29 April 2012

I have often stated that several major components are missing from modern Hermetic practices—the stress here being on the word MODERN—and that these need to be reintroduced if Hermeticism is to take its place as a useful system of philosophy, theosophy, and as a source of gnosis for modern men and women.

In several previous articles ("How to Acquire Occult Power," "Order Out of Chaos," and "A Perfect Practice for the Age of Destruction"), some methods were suggested that can allow modern students of Hermeticism to connect to the mindstream of classical Hermeticism and thereby awaken themselves to the true nature of mind—or Being—as expressed in the classical teachings.

Among the most important points made concerned *altruism*, the desire to "learn in order to serve" as it was at one time called or, in the Vow of the Awakened Heart, to become Illuminated for the sake of all thinking beings so that we can assist in their awakening and thereby bring an end to the suffering they experience as a result of ignorance.

Achieving the first part of this Awakening or Illumination is often called "Knowledge and Conversation" with one's "Holy Guardian Angel," to use the language of Abramelin made famous by Aleister Crowley. It is also known as one's Agathodaimon, or "Good Daemon," in the Hermetic texts.

To achieve this awakening, many modern students use one or more variations of the so-called "Bornless Ritual" (or prayer) found in the *Goetia* (*Lesser Key of Solomon*) translated by S. L. M. Mathers, edited and introduced by Crowley.[1] More importantly, in *Hermetic Magic: The Postmodern Magical Papyrus of Abaris*, edited and introduced by Stephen Edred Flowers, Ph.D.,[2] Flowers provides a more accurate translation of this famous prayer: the Rite of the Headless One.[3]

Readers familiar with the above prayer, however, will notice it is similar to the following prayer from Poimandres, Book One of the Hermetica:

> Holy is God, the Father of All, who is before the first
>   beginning;
> Holy is God, whose purpose is accomplished by his
>   several powers;
> Holy is God, who wills to be known, and is known
>   by them that are his own.
>
> Holy art Thou, who by thy Word created all that is;
> Holy art Thou, whose brightness nature has not dark-
>   ened;
> Holy art Thou, of whom all nature is an image.
> Holy art Thou, who are stronger than all domina-
>   tion...
>
> Accept pure offerings of speech from a soul and heart
>   uplifted to thee, Thou of whom no words can tell,
>   no tongue can speak, only silence can declare.

---

[1] S. L. M. Mathers (trans.), Aleister Crowley (ed.), & Hymeneus Beta (ed.), *The Goetia: The Lesser Key of Solomon the King* (York Beach, ME: Weiser, 1995) 5-13.

[2] *Op. cit.*; based in part upon the *Greek Magical Papyrus in Translation*, edited by Pfr. Hans Dieter Betz (Chicago: University of Chicago Press, 1986).

[3] See pp. 182-84 of *Hermetic Magic*.

> I pray that I may never fall away from that knowledge
> of thee which matches with our being. Grant Thou
> my prayer. *And put power into me, that so, having
> obtained this gift, I may enlighten those of my
> race who are in ignorance, my brothers and thy
> sons.*

> Wherefore I believe and bear witness that I enter into
> Life and Light...[4]

The important point here is the second-to-last sentence, "having obtained this gift, I may enlighten those of my race who are in ignorance, my brothers and thy sons." It is here that we see the true reason we are to seek Illumination: so that we can remove ignorance from ourselves and to help others as well. Far too often this notion of assisting others, of being a beacon on the hill, is forgotten or even ignored in contemporary settings, or worse yet, mutilated into some kind of political statement or call for social action.

Students who have not read the classical Hermetic texts, or even excerpts with commentaries on them, are also unfamiliar with the role visualization plays in classical meditation. In the post "How to Acquire Occult Power," a somewhat lengthy but simple visualization practice was given to assist students in creating the needed psychic space within themselves to attune to the diverse energies of the cosmos, as well as to awaken their sense of interconnectedness, compassion for all beings visible and invisible, and finally to center themselves in the cosmos and the cosmos in their heart—the true seat of mind or consciousness in classical thought.

Similar practices were used in the classical period, and can be read in a passage by Plotinus in his essay, "On Intelligible Beauty" (which can be found in *Thrice-Greatest Hermes: Studies in Hellenistic Theosophy and Gnosis* by G. R. S. Mead), where he states:

---

[4]Cf. Clement Salaman, et al., *op. cit.*, 24. Emphasis added.

Let us then form a mental image of this cosmos with each of its parts remaining what it is, and yet interpenetrating one another, [imagining] them all together into one as much as we possibly can—so that whatsoever comes first into the mind as the "one" [or first sphere], there immediately follows also the sight and semblance of the sun...the other stars [planets]...the earth, sea, and all living things, as though in one transparent sphere...as though all things could be seen in it.

...holding this sphere in the mind, conceive in thy self another sphere removing [from it all ideas of physical] mass; take from it also [the idea of] space, and the phantoms of matter from thy mind... Then invoking God, who hath made [that true sphere] of which you hold the image [phantom] in your mind, pray that He may come. And He may come with his own cosmos, with all the Gods therein—He being one and all, and each one united into one, yet different in their powers, and yet, in that one power of multitude all are One...[5]

Students should compare this to the instructions often given in Tibetan yoga for (1) the imagination of the body prior to *tummo* (Inner Fire) practices; (2) the offerings of the mandala, or world image; (3) the foundational notion of inherent emptiness upon which all Buddhist teachings and practices are based.

It is in foundational practices such as this that true and genuine power, compassion, and Illumination are attained, as it is in this fundamental understanding of our interconnectedness AND the foundational transience of all phenomena—be it mental, emotional, psychic, or physical (as stated in Ecclesiastes [3:1], "For everything there is a season")—can we

---

[5]G. R. S. Mead, *Thrice-Greatest Hermes: Studies in Hellenistic Theosophy and Gnosis*, Vol. I (London: Theosophical Publishing Society, 1906) 252.

come to master our own mind. It is mastery of Mind that is
de facto mastery of self or Being. This is what Hermeticism
is all about. Occult practices, be they divination, evocation,
alchemical transmutation, or simple healing, are based on the
fact that all apparent reality is in fact rooted in an underlying "nothingness" or non-specific energy-mind that unites,
gives rise to, supports, brings change to, and reabsorbs all
that is. Our mind is one with this mind, our mind *is* this
mind, and when we step back and allow that unity to rise up
and experience it, we have Illumined or Awakened moments.
When we learn to actively enter into the centered still point
of mind, we can then become conscious creators of our inner
and outer worlds, and not unconscious prisoners of the Law of
Causation, Karma, or Cause and Result. We then understand
why the ancient mysteries were *cosmological* in nature, yet
stated that our fundamental duty is to "Know Thyself" and,
from this, realize that "God is man, and man is God, and
there is no God but Man." Understand yourself as microcosm,
and the macrocosm will open itself to you.

Morality and Ethics in Esotericism

5 February 2008

While it is generally agreed that our outer health (even material circumstances) are a direct reflection of our inner wholeness, in practice, the connection of this idea in reality is a lot less simple for many. Much if not all of this difficulty comes from the notion that esotericism is a sort of "do it yourself" process in which practitioners can "pick what they like and leave the rest behind." In reality, while that is fine to tell drug addicts and alcoholics (who are on the edge of total self-destruction, so anything is better than nothing) in an NA or AA meeting, it is a lie when it comes to teaching students who "of their own free will and accord" have placed themselves on a path of illumination.

In *Kabbalah for Health and Wellness*[1] there is a discussion of the role of the Ten Commandments (plus the two given by Jesus) in psychological and physical health, so that inner realizations could take place. Somehow the knee-jerk rejection of anything rooted in Western culture took sway, and some Neopagans reviewing the book seemed bent on criticizing this point rather than taking a step back and remembering that Kabbalah is essentially Jewish, even when it is dressed up in late-nineteenth and early twentieth century polytheistic and reconstructionist metaphors. You can throw the baby

---

[1]Mark Stavish, *Kabbalah for Health and Wellness: Second Revised & Updated Edition* (Institute for Hermetic Studies, 2017).

out with the bathwater, but in the end, you are left holding an empty bucket.

This desire to strip traditional teachings of any connection to their past is by no means limited to studies of Kabbalah. American Buddhists are notorious for it as well. Like their Leftist, counter-culture, Sixties holdovers in the Neopagan community, American Buddhists find it nearly impossible to sit down, shut up, listen, and change their point of view—even if for a moment—but instead insist on picking and choosing what moral and ethical precepts they like and which ones they don't like. This is especially true when it comes to teachings against sodomy and sexual license in general, and it is further extended into the need to turn everything into a political and social movement rather than to do the hard work of deconstructing and reconstructing themselves as individuals. It is as if the idea of actually being an individual—even for a moment—is too frightening to their entrenched collectivist ideology. "If it is good enough for me, then it is good enough for everyone," seems to be the motto of too many pathological reforms across many of the current spiritual groups in the United States, Europe, and the Middle East.

Within Buddhism and its Tibetan predecessor, Bön, there are Ten Virtuous Deeds. Like the Ten Commandments for those who practice Kabbalah in any of its forms (Christian or Hermetic), the Ten Virtuous Deeds are not an option—they must be strictly followed.

The Ten Virtuous Deeds are:

1. Avoiding taking another's life, including animal and plant beings whenever possible.
2. Practicing generosity.
3. Being mindful, paying attention to what you are doing and what you are thinking of at any moment.
4. Following moral discipline to overcome sexual misconduct.
5. Telling the truth and avoiding falsehood.
6. Working to bring together friends who have separated,

and not spreading rumors.

7. Speaking peacefully and calmly and avoiding harsh language.
8. Practicing prayer, meditation, pilgrimages, and other works, rather than wasting time, particularly on gossip.
9. Being free of evil thoughts toward others, generating love and kindness toward them rather than harmful thoughts.
10. Being free from wrong views of the teachings one is receiving, particularly: firmly realizing the truth of the law of karma (cause and result or effect) and firmly entering the spiritual pathway.

If we take a careful look at these non-optional moral and ethical requirements, we can see that they are in fact even more stringent than the so-called Ten Commandments found in Jewish scripture and adopted by the Christians. The Ten Commandments can be summarized by: put God first, don't blaspheme, keep one day set aside for spiritual practice, don't steal, don't kill, don't lie, don't commit adultery, and don't desire for what another person owns. The Egyptian Negative Confession to Truth or Maat is even more detailed, yet repeats the same themes. All of these guidelines are direct and to the point—if you want to know God, or experience enlightenment, then these are the rules you need to follow. And if these are too burdensome, your journey will become a longer and more difficult one. The choice is up to you.

The simple truth is that only by following such guidelines—*particularly* when it is difficult, when it causes material or social loss, and goes against the predisposed ego (self-pitying and self-limiting) image we cherish of ourselves—can we really say we are on the Path. Only with a firm commitment to organize our inner life and master the inner energies that run rampant within our psyche can we hope to be open to deeper realizations and experiences we call *spiritual*, as well as to project that new-found harmony as power and form in the material world.

We can either treat genuine and authentic spiritual teachings as a rich multi-course meal that has been laid out for us by a master chef and staff...or we can treat it like a buffet where we indulge our preferences and walk away having paid too much money for second or third rate food, only to get indigestion.

For Western esotericism to survive and thrive in its own soil it must provide solid evidence that it is more than just a collection of occult and psychic thrill seekers, but has *real* and *tangible* means of living a healthy and happy life. Morality and ethics are the beginning and end of who we are and the litmus test of our spiritual path, for this shows how we treat others and ourselves.

Is Western Esotericism Dead?

9 April 2012

I was recently asked the question "Is Western esotericism dead?" I replied, "No—it is on life support." This was followed up by a request for clarification, to which I gave the following details. If we look at the history of esotericism in the West (that is Europe and North America) we notice several things.

First, esotericism is just that: esoteric. Something that has remained hidden. In fact, to speak of Western esotericism is in a way to be redundant. That is, the manner in which esotericism grew in Western culture is unique to it, as it is in those areas outside of Europe where Christian influence was established as the religious litmus test of the day.

To be clear, we can speak of a school of esoteric Tibetan Buddhism, but in truth, the word "esoteric" does not hold the same meaning or weight. In Oriental cultures, even within Islamic lands at various places and times (although it too suffers from the weight of rigid Abrahamic monotheism), there was and still is the collective religious practices of the community, peculiar local or family variations that may exist, personal practices that link the two, and (if one desires it) further religious training available. This training is mainly concerned with moral and ethical activities, as well as fundamental training of the mind to be open to spiritual realities.

The pathway to this training is well known and established. It is not hidden, and for the most part it is open to anyone. Even in those instances where extreme poverty, lack of education, or other obstacles prevent one from furthering one's spiritual education, wandering teachers, monks, magicians, healers, and even local laypersons fill the void and are accessible. In short, there is a culture of spirituality that is well established and widely known. Some teachings may be hard to find, but it is generally known that they exist, and often local variations exist that can be accessed.

A perfect example of this is what is widely known in the West as Tibetan yoga, or tantra, which was in fact widely known in Tibet (prior to the Chinese genocide) but not widely practiced. It is generally stated that only about 10% of the monks in Tibet practiced tantra, with most of them being content to recite prayers, spin prayer wheels, perform rituals, and undertake the more general day-to-day monastic practices. Yet even so, in a country where up to 20% of the population was professionally involved in religious and spiritual practices, this meant that maybe as many as 150,000 — 200,000 people were involved in the practice of tantra! In short, somehow, somewhere, be it in a monastery, hermitage, or cave, there was someone who could teach you if you really wanted to learn.

In the West, secrecy was forced upon the various esoteric traditions by an intolerant religious-political system. Secret societies grew up out of necessity rather than by design. Small groups at best could practice and learn from a single teacher, and discussion with others, or knowing about others on the Path, was nearly impossible. Open debate, comparison, and discussion of methods, results, theories, and practices was nonexistent. Fear and secrecy ruled and dominated the major decisions of the majority of people involved in esoteric activities up until a generation or two ago.

As a second point, much of this notion of secrecy has become so embedded in the thinking of leaders, teachers, and students of various schools and practices, that they think it is normal because it is "tradition," and forget the reasons why it came about. Many will claim that it is to "protect the teachings." When asked, "Protect them from what?" the answer is usually pretty lame. Often it is said from abuse or misuse, while at the same time claiming that results can only come if one is spiritually open enough. This contradiction is ignored, and all that is really being protected is the real lack of knowledge and experience that many of the self-appointed defenders of the "traditions" really have.

This, coupled with outright fraud, infighting, libel, slander, and vile personality attacks has left many in Western esotericism saying, "Okay, these people are human and it is not about personality, it is about the teachings."

But my point, and that of those who raise these questions to me, is this: if the teachings are to make one a better person, then either those who engage in these behaviors are not practicing what they teach, or the teachings themselves are false.

The most often-raised example of this is the methods of the Hermetic Order of the Golden Dawn. We need only look at the activities of the Order's founders to ask ourselves some serious questions about the efficacy of the methods. All of those banishings clearly did little for Mathers, Crowley, and others. French and other European orders and their American spawn are no better off. If it were not for the Internet, most would not even have a presence in the world other than their P.O. Box and the rubber stamps they use to make documents "official." The paper-trading scam of cross-initiation, validation, and recognition is well known. Most have been trading around the same sad set of photocopies for twenty years or more, secretly hoping to become the next AMORC while using it as their combined online whipping post and recruiting ground for new members. The running joke about the various Gnostic churches is that they are all bishops and no congregations, and their chapel is always someone's living room with the sofa pushed against the wall, or another rented hotel conference room.

As a result of this lack of trust and confidence in the

leaders and teachers of contemporary esotericism, many have turned to it and look upon it as a commodity, something that one buys regardless of the source or salesman selling it to you. It may be true that my mechanic, lawyer, or physician need not be saintly to do their job well, but when it comes to esotericism what we entrust our well-being to is incarnate in the character of the person before us that we see as a teacher.

I would like to quote two paragraphs from some lectures dating back to the 1920s and earlier. Please consider the following when doing your meditations on Kether, as well as during practice of the Lesser Ritual of the Pentagram:

> ...you will find that the circle, with its dot, becomes not only a symbol but a real and practical thing, because through development, and through exercises which you may receive...through study and practice, you are enabled in times of trouble and when in serious situations, mental, physical, and spiritual, to draw a mystic circle around yourself while you become the dot in the circle, and no vibrations of an unpleasant nature, no harm or trouble can break through that mystic circle and reach you. This mystic circle can even become luminous and quite visible in a dark room. It is one means of great protection and as the mystic stands in the center of his circle he is in the center of a temporarily created universe of his own in which he has omnipotent power for the time being, and sees and knows all things independent of all other means of cognition.[1]

Also, from Éliphas Lévi, the French Rosicrucian:

> The destiny of man, as we have said, is to make or create himself; he is and will be the son of his works, both for time and eternity. All men are called into the lists, but the number of the elect, that is, of those who

---

[1]Harvey Spencer Lewis (1927).

succeed, is invariably small. In other words, the men
who are desirous to attain are numbered by multitude,
but the chosen are few. Men who are masters of
themselves become easily the masters of others; but
it is possible for them to hinder one another if they
disregard the laws of discipline and of the universal
hierarchy. Life is a warfare in which we must give
proofs if we would advance; power does not surrender
itself; it must be seized. Initiation by contest and
ordeal is therefore indispensable for the attainment
of the practical science of mysticism. The essential law
of nature, that of initiation by effort and by voluntary
and toilsome progress, has been misconstrued fatally.[2]

I hope these words are of inspiration and illumination to
you on your Path.

As we have stated clearly, and repeated every so often
for those new to my writing, contemporary spirituality is
a commercial enterprise and little more. When something
is no longer profitable, authors and publishers move on to
other subjects, for that is the nature of publishing. Only
those groups or individuals that utilize Print On Demand
services or self-publish through some other mechanism can
afford to, or have the option of, keeping something available
to a limited market because it is viewed as an important
work or for sentimental reasons. Publishers and authors need
to eat as well, and it takes sales for that to happen. Along
these lines, book sales across the board are in decline as we
enter into the final phase of idiot culture with the notion that
we can "multimedia" the spiritual unfoldment of a human
being. It is a pity that those who hawk these wares fail to
understand or care that for them to work there need to be
cheap, available resources and disposable income to purchase
them with, often at inflated prices. This also requires the

---

[2]Éliphas Lévi (trans. A. E. Waite), *Transcendental Magic: Its Doctrine and Ritual* (York Beach, ME: Samuel Weiser, Inc., 1995) 267, 270-71.

continued use of and access to the technology required to run it, and the power to do so.

In the end, the book has always been the principal manner of preserving and transmitting esoteric teachings, even if only in rudimentary form. However, to assist in this, someone with some experience in the practices contained in the book, as well as their own inner journey, is required to help each person make progress as well.

SPIRITUAL
GROUPS
AND
SERVICE

Karma Yoga 2.0

25 March 2015

As many of you are aware, there are four forms of traditional yoga—Jñana, Bhakti, Raja, and Karma—that form the foundation for the various yogic practices. These four areas are the means of practice that we can use to achieve union with our ideal and, thereby, come to spiritual awakening. Jñana Yoga is realization through study that reveals to us wisdom. Bhakti Yoga is realization through devotion to an ideal, be it in the form of the teacher (hence the practice of Guru Yoga) or an idea, giving rise to many of the missionary forms of religious and spiritual practice. Raja Yoga is the methodical study of the mind as well as karma, or "cause and effect." It is directly experiential and aimed, like a laser beam, at the very essence of being. While Jñana Yoga uses our intellect as the tool for awakening, Bhakti Yoga uses our emotions, with Raja Yoga using the nature of mind itself and Karma Yoga using the body and its effects as the tool and the path.

Karma Yoga is described as the "yoga of work." This means that the person undertaking Karma Yoga consciously takes on a task as a means of furthering the illumination of themselves, and that of others, even though the fruits from that labor will be very material in their expression. For example, it is very common for attendees at a Buddhist retreat center to pay their daily fees for room, board, and teachings, and still undertake a variety of chores to maintain the facility.

Cutting grass, helping prepare meals, doing building maintenance, and cleaning the temple are all aspects of Karma
Yoga. Some will even list it on their retreat schedules as such.

However, for those who cannot attend these kinds of
events, but still wish to support their teacher, lodge, or school
in some fashion, what can they do? Technology has made
volunteering easier, particularly in the area of creating publications, videos, and educational tools. Reliable international
shipping is also a powerful tool for the creation, transporta-
tion, and utilization of various ritual tools, works of art, and
highly rare and valuable specialty items connected to the
Work. Thus, it is very easy for someone in Thailand to send
me, in the eastern United States of America, several pounds
of antimony for alchemical work, or for someone in Europe
to send rare esoteric texts. Modern technology has freed us
from the need to be physically present, or even within a few
hours' distance, to be of assistance to the spiritual teachers,
groups, and movements that help us on our Path of Return.

This ease is not without its own problems, however; the
principal issue is that "ease of contact" equals "superficiality
of contact" (or, as the saying goes, "easy come, easy go"). It
is not uncommon for esoteric relationships to be more like
serial dating than courtships. Everything is hot and heavy in
the beginning, and then as reality sets in, the need to keep
the emotional and sexual intensity at an all-time high kicks
in, and off the student goes, to a new lover: a new teacher,
school, or path.

For those who *do* stay and develop a meaningful, healthy,
and mature relationship with their teachers and fellow students, the path becomes very much like marriage with its ups
and downs but, for the most part, both parties are in it until
the end. This means that both parties demonstrate respect for
what the other's role is in the relationship. While clearly not
a relationship of equals—at least not for a while—each knows
that the other brings something meaningful and needed to
the other party. Yet the needs must be proportional the roles

and responsibilities.

If the teacher needs to teach, more than the student needs to learn, then the relationship is doomed from the start. If this is the case, the student does not have a mature individual as a spiritual friend, guide, and drill instructor, but, instead, an individual who so desperately needs the approval of others that the only way they can find it is through the highly subjective world of appearing knowledgeable about "spirituality." I know this sounds harsh, but that is the way it is. For the first few years, the student must desire the company of the teacher, a company that can be at times very demanding and even torturous, more than the teacher needs whatever it is the student brings to them. For in the beginning, all the student can bring is their body, their wealth, and the promise or potential of it being forged into a tool of awakening.

In one of her writings on Tibetan Buddhism, Janet Gyatso stated, "Lamas need adoring students." I think this is very true, and it can also be said for many involved in Western esoteric movements as well. It provides a fresh impetus to the teachings and motivation to the teacher. Students who are too enamored with their teacher are really unable to understand this, as they cannot see through their own projections long enough to glimpse the truth. At some point, too many teachers are unwilling to remove the glamour, to pull back the curtain so reality can be glimpsed, as it has a proven track record of negatively impacting the year-end financial statements. Instead, students find their attention and energies being overtly and excessively directed toward building and construction projects, outreach, and (of course) the proselytizing and fundraising activities that accompany them.

This is not to condemn planning, growth, and maintenance programs, but to point out that these are but one-quarter of the work, and that devotion to the ideal, the teacher, and the teachings represented is but one-quarter of the work. The remaining *half* of our work is personal study and practice. It is this half that is really most critical, as it is in theory the reason we are attracted to spiritual work to begin with. Only when combined do these four qualities or means of practice give a balance and harmony to one's individual growth while simultaneously supporting the teacher, group, or lodge.

How Much Is Enough?

Two hours a week in volunteer work is about 2½ weeks of volunteer time a year. One hour a week would be half of that. So, if you are leading a study group, preparing for one or two events a year, or assisting in ongoing maintenance, this would easily absorb that time. In this case, one could say their Karma Yoga duties are fulfilled. If one is contributing a sum of money equal to one or two weeks of earnings (after taxes is fine), that would also be a fulfillment of one's sense of Karma Yoga. At an income of $50,000 per year, that would be a donation of approximately $600 and $1,200 per year, or $50 to $100 per month over and above whatever one's annual dues or affiliation costs. Of course, one is free to figure out whatever percentage for donating they like—the amount is used for illustration.

This leads us to the important point of how to know if we are overextending ourselves.

1. Is your involvement affecting your ability to pay your bills?
2. Is your involvement encouraging you to do more so that you can express and become more in your personal life, or is it all aimed at the teacher or group?
3. Is the group encouraging involvement to the detriment of your personal practice?
4. Is the ideal of self-sacrifice held out over self-expression of our talents and deepest potential?
5. Do you enjoy what you are doing for the group?

6. Do you volunteer because you want to help and support, or out of a sense of pressure or the desire to be recognized as being special?
7. What would you do with your time and resources if you were *not* supporting the teacher, group, or lodge?

While not exhaustive, the above questions are meant to focus our attention on the "why" of our group involvement and support rather than the "how." In the end, the "how" is about the sustainability of the organization. This sustainability is either through direct cash donations, money raised through recruitment or fundraising, or savings on cash expenditures from members donating their services.

So, while we are not asking you to put a price tag on everything you do, we are asking you to recognize the cost of your involvement so that you can make healthy and positive choices that move your spiritual practice forward and do not side-track or even derail it.

This also means you need to know what you get in return for your efforts.

1. Does this get you some sense of importance?
2. Easier access to the Lama or Guru?
3. Promotion in the ranks?
4. What is the actual benefit or lessons learned that you receive from volunteering for your organization or movement of choice?

Be careful about false promises such as special initiations, wealth rituals or practices, audiences with dignitaries, a new funny hat, or a better seat at the table. The worst of lies, however, is when we are told that our work and sacrifice will be witnessed by the Unseen Masters, the Unknown Superiors, and we will be rewarded by them at some future date and time. Such are bribes aimed at increasing one's sense of self-importance rather than genuine signs of spiritual awakening. The two can go together, but it is rare and difficult to find them paired. In short, we must work and volunteer because we *want* to, and not because we feel we "must" or "need" to participate in such a manner.

This also means we need to take a good hard look at our relationship to the teacher, the teachings, and the community of which we are a member. It does not exist for us alone, and if we treat it as a commodity, that is fine, but then do not be surprised if in return we are not allowed entrance without having bought our ticket.

So, look at your involvement with your teachers, teachings, and community of practitioners and ask yourself if you have a healthy or unhealthy relationship with them. Are you pulling your own weight and ensuring the health and continuity of the movement for future generations? Is your idealism and altruism being abused under the guise of self-sacrifice and service to the greater good? Or as one fellow likes to remind me, is the phrase and idealism of Karma Yoga being used as a euphemism for "indentured servitude"?

As stated in *Light on the Path: A Study Guide for Qabala, Alchemy & Astrology*,[1] no one ever tells a volunteer when to stop, so remember that it is all right to say "No" when asked to do something. Volunteering of one's time, talent, and treasure must be done freely, otherwise it is coercion and conscription and whatever good that can be achieved by it is already limited. Encourage but do not force or pressure others to help in whatever way they can. This way, each will find their right place at "the Table of the Lord."

---

[1]Mark Stavish, *Light on the Path: A Study Guide for Qabala, Alchemy & Astrology* (IHS Study Guide Vol. I, 2014).

Karma and Deficit Spending

13 January 2013

In response to recent posts regarding karma, I was asked the question, "How can we objectively measure our karma?" In truth, so much of karma is subjective—that is, its true alchemical tincture goes on within our own mind—that it can be difficult at times to know where our mind is taking us. However, there is a simple test we can take, an accounting measure if you will, that will let us know if we are investing in the future or if we are deficit spending in the karma department.

Now, the following is not just an abstract notion. You are encouraged to actually sit down and do this, not just for today, but for several days, to get the cold, hard facts on what kind of future you are really creating with your mind.

1. Take a sheet of paper and a pen or pencil and write down the topics that dominate your thinking, even if just for this morning.
2. After each one write down how much time you spent on it, even if just a few seconds or a minute or two.
3. Write down a "P" if the emotions created were positive (that is, loving, kind, hopeful, supportive of others, encouraging, or generous).
4. Write down an "N" if the emotions created were negative (that is, angry, frustrating, hateful, selfish, self-pitying, destructive, or disheartening).

5. Add up the total time spent on "P" and, in a separate column, the total time spent on "N." You may have some thoughts that are neutral or indifferent, but on close inspection, you will notice that, for many, even the weather creates an emotional response, so be honest with yourself.

6. Now, if the positive column is bigger than the negative column you are "in the black." If the negative column is bigger than the positive column, you are "in the red" and deficit spending on your karma.

7. If the columns are about the same size, or the positive is only slightly bigger, then your profit margin is slim, and you may not have enough reserves to ride out any surprises that life may bring to you.

8. So, take a long and serious look at the Negative Column and make a conscious decision to bring that down to a manageable size, while at the same time increasing the Positive Column.

In short, pay attention to your own mind, to what you are thinking and where it is ultimately taking you. This is the basis of all esoteric practices whose goal is illumination or enlightenment.

This may sound silly, but I look forward to hearing from each of you who have actually done this for a week or two— or better, a month or two—as it will show in clear and decisive terms where each of our lives is heading and that we, ultimately, are the creators of it.

Tantra, Traditions, and Trust

17 September 2015

Over the last twenty-four hours I have received a host of emails and Facebook posts from people regarding my statements yesterday about building traditions, infrastructure, and leaving something for tomorrow's generations. The most common theme mentioned was concern over hucksters and shameless opportunists who exploit the situation.

Well, they have always existed and always will. One must learn the virtue of discernment and, with that, the ability to trust those we go to for assistance in our Work of Becoming. This is the first lesson on the Path of Return: learning discrimination. So, to reply in short order, I am quoting B. Bhattacharya, author of *The World of Tantra* and other titles on the same topic. Shiva tantric practices have maintained an unbroken series of lineages, places of worship, and holy sites for millennia. This experienced tantric practitioner of old India states,

> Liberation is not acquired merely for idling or vegetating.
>
> Liberation's power is elemental. Liberation is a birth-right to be acquired more spiritually than politically. One must feel free as the elements: the air, the sky, the light and heat from the sun, the rains and the sound. One must feel natural. The elements as well as the yogi relate their power to the source,

the cosmos. Thus they are able to derive their power from the Cosmic Source. A man of God receives to distribute; takes to give back; exists to bestow; works to serve. A man of God follows principles to maintain the balance of form and order.[1]

Thus, if I ask of you more than you ask from yourselves it is for these reasons. If you trust your teachers, then you have no problem doing as they ask or assisting to the best of your ability in their work. If you do not believe your teacher to be, in the author's words, "a man of God" but just "a man," that is fine. But if you do not trust him or her, then it is time to walk away.

To this same end, I encourage each of you reading this to walk away from this book if you do not believe in or desire to support with your time, talent, or treasure our Work. We ask of you to give to us so that we can give back in return, not just to you but to others as well. Again, to use the author's words, "receives to distribute; takes to give back...to maintain the balance of form and order." We ask that you expand your sense of possibilities, and both trust in and support our Work. For if you do not, then why stay? Find a person, place, and ideal that you can put your time, talent, and treasure into and derive the benefits from such affiliation. That will then be the best path for your Becoming.

---

[1]Brajamadhava Bhattacharya, *The World of Tantra* (Delhi [India]: Munshiram Manoharlal Pub., 1988) 222.

Teach Your Children Well

2 April 2016

Recently a host of emails, threads, and even book reviews have been sent to me by readers that all focus around the question: what makes for a good spiritual teacher? This question is particularly relevant as increasingly we seem to have divorced the notion of spirituality—and by this I am specifically speaking about ritual magic and alchemy—from any real inner transformation. That is, we look at them as technical subjects that can be taught, like algebra, welding, or accounting, without any relationship between the subject and the character of the teacher.

In short, there exists a notion that a person of questionable morality and ethics can be a "good spiritual teacher" while being a "bad person"; that it is possible for someone to be on the Path of Return, experiencing Illumination and Knowledge and Conversation with their Holy Guardian Angel, yet still from this privileged position treat others within as well as outside of the esoteric community abusively. Somehow we are willing to accept this kind of rationale in occult circles while hypocritically condemning it in religious circles. We call for the imprisonment of the head of the Roman Catholic Archdiocese of Philadelphia for his role in covering up the rape of children, yet we are all too willing to accept lesser (though no less egregious) crimes from our own magical guides—from people who presumably "know better."

Now to be fair, most esoteric organizations are not in a position where the care of children is given to them. Most of their adherents are adults, and when children are involved they are part of a wider activity. The point, however, is still relevant: am I willing to trust you with my children? If not, then why would I trust you with my mind or soul? Now insert any other noun in place of "children" and read the question again. "Am I willing to trust you with my wife, money, dog, or houseplants? If not, why would I trust you with my mind or soul?"

You see, in the opening stages of a relationship with our potential spiritual "friend and guide" it is important that we ask this question. Trust is the basis for all relationships, and all the more so in the domain of the mind, wherein we must have total confidence that our teacher has our best interests at heart and is truly following the Golden Rule. If that trust is abused or broken by the teacher, untold damage is created. If that trust is not held tight by the student, then the more difficult areas of the path will be harder to navigate, if they can be navigated at all.

In *Kabbalah for Health and Wellness*,[1] and in the audio program *Unfolding the Rose: Illumination & Western Esotericism*[2] three supports were mentioned as being critical to the journey.

> ...three Outer Essentials are also required, these consist of the Teacher, the Teachings, and our Companions. As mentioned in *Kabbalah for Health and Wellness*, these can easily be seen in the Three Greater Lights of the Masonic Lodge, wherein there is the Master (Teacher), the Volume of the Sacred Law (Teachings), and the Lodge members (Companions),

---

[1]Mark Stavish, *Kabbalah for Health and Wellness: Second Revised & Updated Edition* (IHS Publications, 2017).

[2]See the IHS YouTube Channel. See also the lecture transcriptions given in Mark Stavish, *Unfolding the Rose: Illumination & Western Esotericism* (IHS Study Guide Vol. V, 2017).

also known as "the Household of the Faithful." In Hermeticism, we see the reference to "adoption" as the entering into a close teacher and student relationship of an intimate nature that mingles the minds similar to the mingling of bloodlines through the adoption process, thereby making one a formal member of the initiatic chain of transmission.

Teacher: Knowledge of the teachings, demonstrated practice, and ability to transmit both the academic and practical aspects clearly and concisely.

Teachings: Valid source, proven efficacy, and intact written and/or verbal transmissions.

Companions: Those who have gone before, those who go with us, and those who will come after us on the Path of Return.

Later on it was stated:

In summary we can say that there are five questions we must satisfy ourselves with:

1. What is the purpose of the teachings?
2. What is the source of the teachings?
3. What does the Path involve from beginning to end?
4. What can I expect from the Work? What will the results be?
5. How does this Path compare to other paths and methods?

If one is having trouble with the answers to these questions, then it is possible to reduce it even further; remember the Gospel, "By their fruits ye shall know them."[3] Look at the

---

[3]Matthew 7:16.

teacher, the teachings, and the body of practitioners and ask yourself: "Are these decent, trustworthy human beings? Do their Thoughts, Words, and Deeds form a harmonious whole, or are they incongruous? Are they kind, generous, polite, and strong? Or are they argumentative, arrogant, competitive, and domineering? Or, more simply, would you trust your children with them? Even if they would not physically rape your child, would you want your child exposed to their actions and values, to, in effect, grow up and become like them?"

These are important questions, since the role of teachers in Western esotericism continues to change, as do the people who take on that role. In the end, it is your child you are protecting and nurturing, be it your inner child or your genetic offspring. Guard them well.

ON
EVIL

A Strange Little Exorcism

19 May 2016

I was out running errands yesterday when I ran into one of the leaders of a local paranormal investigating team. He said, "How are you doing? I haven't seen you in months and now—just after your name comes up we meet."

So I asked, "Who was talking about me? Something scandalous I hope."

He laughed and said, "No, it was good. I heard you did a job for someone. A sachet. They said it worked really well." I did not correct him, as "sachet" is the common name for what I made. In Pennsylvania German folklore it is called a *brauche bag* or pow-wow bag. It is functionally the same as a mojo bag in hoodoo and conjure practices.

I looked down and collected myself. "Yes, if it is the one I am thinking of, then that was some much-needed work. An intervention really. I rarely interfere in other people's business, but that was multi-generational. Some kind of strange haunting attached to the female side of the family. It was going to end badly, so I had to try something. They clearly wanted help, but—like nearly everyone in that situation—did not know how to get it or what to do."

He nodded in agreement, having seen many similar instances himself. Having found what I was looking for in the store aisle, I concluded our meeting with a warm thanks and wished him luck in some upcoming activities.

I write this because it is important to know that opportunities to help others arise if we are open to them. It is also critical to realize that we can only help those who want it. Studies have shown that people who believe in the power of prayer, who ask for prayer in their lives, or any other form of assistance that relies heavily on the power of positive thinking benefit from it even when it is performed for them by others. This is not to limit this kind of activity to a kind of materialistic internal phenomena, as the results in psychosomatic medicine are too dramatic to simply say, "It's all in your head," and believe it stays there. No, the mind and body (and with this our personal environment) are deeply connected. But, we can only help those who want to help themselves. This is why we hear in the Gospel Jesus saying, "Your faith has made you well."

In this case it was not a physical illness that was being addressed, but a mental one—not in the typical sense of mental illness, but in the sense that what was happening in the lives of those involved was primarily a phenomena of the mind. This does not mean it was "all in their heads" but, rather, that what we think of as "spiritual" and "paranormal" is primarily a mental phenomena. That is why it has become labeled a function of the Sixth Sense. There are many ways to bring the mind to ease, and with it, the body, and the surrounding environment as well. Once that is accomplished, happiness can grow, for there will be no room for sorrow, in the mind as well as in the environment.

The methods used are in part discussed in *The Inner Way:*

The Power of Prayer & Belief in Spiritual Practice,[1] and are explored in detail in our YouTube series entitled "Pow-Wow: Traditional Folk & Grimoire Magic."[2]

Illness and Psychic Parasites

Unseen Hazards of the Healthcare Professions

20 May 2016

After my last post entitled "A Strange Little Exorcism," I received, as would be expected, several emails from people. One of them came from one of our long-time supporters and patrons. Below is his description and interpretation of events regarding a patient in his healthcare practice.

Dear Mark,

I am passing this on to you so that you may share it with your readers.

As a healthcare professional my primary focus is in traditional Chinese medicine. This is important because in classical medicine we take the idea of "chi sickness," or what is often referred to as "wind disorder" in Tibetan medicine, very seriously. Chi (or prana), as you know, is similar—and in some instances identical to—the *pneuma* of classical Hermeticism. It is the energy of life and consciousness.

That said, I have a patient who over the last few months I have grown to dislike. I simply dreaded seeing her and I did not know why. She is a soon-to-be retired teacher, non-practicing Jew, leaning

---

[1]Mark Stavish, *The Inner Way: The Power of Prayer & Belief in Spiritual Practice* (IHS Study Guide Vol. II, 2014).

[2]See the IHS YouTube Channel; also see Mark Stavish, *Pow-Wow: Traditional Folk & Grimoire Magic of the Pennsylvania German Magi* (IHS Study Guide Vol. X, 2017).

towards atheism, and generally grumpy. Well, this is
no surprise, as I guess I would be grumpy if I taught
inner-city high school adolescents all day. Of course
when I see people they are ill, so they are rarely in
the best of moods. But it was more than this.

At her last appointment she told me that she
was diagnosed with Stage Four pancreatic cancer.
Something very profound and miraculous would be
needed to keep her alive. So I decided to do something
a little different with her next appointment to see if
it would help her, or at least make it easier for me
to treat her during her session.

Just prior to her arrival I blessed the room, performed a short ritual of purification, invoked the
archangels, and held in my mind the idea that this
was a safe place for her and myself. I did this with
the belief that my general ill feelings toward her were
a direct response to the energetic parasites that were
feeding off her and her suffering. This was a very brief
ritual and not elaborate by any stretch.

Now, as she is walking down the hallway, she
comes to an abrupt stop three feet from the door to
our normal examination room. She stands straight
up, turns to her left and says, "Can we use this room
instead?"

The room she wanted to enter is a massage ther-
apy room. Its lights were off, door mostly closed, no
music or aromatherapy scents coming from it, and
the lavender walls barely visible. It was, as we say, a
low-energy environment. I asked her why, to which
she replied, "Purple is the color of pancreatic cancer
awareness." Her affect was flat as if she were simply
going through the motions. In my mind I thought it
resembled the way zombies are portrayed. I found
this very interesting and agreed, quickly sanctifying
the room when we entered and continuing to do so
throughout the session.

The exam went well. After she left she was in

better spirits and so was I. Her color had improved
and she was smiling. Given that I had done nothing different, other than the ritual, I feel a certain
confirmation regarding this metaphysical side of the
diagnosis. For myself, the general feeling of irritation
toward her was substantially reduced.

I do not desire to go into the psychoenergetic aspects of the spleen in Chinese medicine (a web search
can do that for readers), but simply want to point
out that I believe my irrational change in attitude
toward my patient was an energetic recognition not
of her disease, but of psychic parasites that were
feeding off her suffering. When I had this realization
and addressed it through ritual and prayer, it was
not until she suddenly stopped and desired to go into
a different room that I became convinced of it. Her
energy was not simply lost to the disease, but she
was being hollowed out from the inside as well.

In Chinese medicine these parasites are sometimes
called *hungry ghosts*, or *GUI*. For those unfamiliar
with it, they eat chi, or life energy, but also the
blood, as that carries the chi, making them sicker. We
rarely talk about this, and certainly not to patients.
However, it is part of the practice, as all Chinese
medicine descends from Wu shamanic practices.

Treating the disease alone is not enough; in classical medicine we must deal with the energetic parasites,
the emotional issues as well, and, most importantly,
helping the patient prepare (in as healthy a state of
mind as possible) for their own death. This does not
mean to give up on the patient and resign them to
the inevitable, but to recognize that in medicine we
are working with death as "inevitable, but just not
yet." The psychological and spiritual well-being of the
patient are in some ways more important—at least
from an Oriental perspective. For us as healthcare and
mental health workers (teachers would be included
as well), we need to take good care of our psycho-

logical and spiritual health. Meditative or ritualistic practices that keep us free of psychic parasites—real or imagined—are extremely important for our overall health when we deal so interactively with the public.

Thank you.

Each of you has experiences that are important to recognize. In conjunction with our writer above, I hope that you have found the sharing of his experiences of value.

Clowns at Midnight

27 August 2013

Several years ago my wife and I were out on a Saturday afternoon. We had just had lunch at a nearby Wendy's—yes, we had the salads—and as I turned down a side road I noticed a sign that read "Estate Sale." I said, "An estate sale. Let's go in."

"What is an estate sale?" she asked.

"Someone dies and the family sells off the contents of the house," I replied.

"So, it is where people wander through to buy a dead person's stuff," she stated, looking at me as she contemplated the various metaphysical permutations of such a situation—or maybe just its creepiness.

"Pretty much. Here's a parking space. Let's go!" I chirped out enthusiastically.

I do not remember much about the contents of the house—it is the *bedroom* that is burned into my brain. There, standing at the edge of the bed, Andrea at my right side, I said, "It gives a whole new meaning to the phrase, 'Clowns are funny, except at midnight.' " The entire bedroom was decorated in clown themes, from the lamp on the bedstand, to various decorations and dolls in every nook and cranny. A fellow bargain hunter walked in, came to a dead stop beside me, made some kind of unintelligible shriek of nightmarish terror and quickly left, heading all the way out the front door.

By this time Andrea had recovered from her shock and asked, "What does that mean, 'Clowns are funny except at midnight'?"

"It means something that is meant to be entertaining can become horrifying under the right conditions. Would you like to wake up to this at 3:00 AM? It also has to do with destroying childhood innocence and trust. Turning something good into evil."

"Clowns freak me out anyhow. This just confirms it. I'm out of here." With that, she left, and there I was, alone in a dead woman's bedroom surrounded by clowns. I think I reached the front door before she did.

Now—fast forward to the present day.

Evil has no sense of humor. It has cynicism, sarcasm, and knowing condescension, but *not* humor, as it takes itself far to seriously for that. You see, humor requires a sense of *fallibility*, being all right with one's vulnerabilities, in short, dignity and self-nurturing that are not confused with pride and vanity.

Evil also does not have love. Now, this should be self-evident, but it needs to be restated. There is a confused sense of self-love we call "pride" and "arrogance," but no real love—not the love of compassion for others and being open to your own weaknesses, along with a willingness to correct them. Pride has only *itself*; arrogance sees no weakness in itself and does not accept it in others—except to prey upon it.

This is important because we do not live in a strictly good and evil world; there is (using the old photographic standards) pure white, pure black, and eight shades of grey in-between. Most of our day is spent in this nebulous world of neither here nor there.

WHY ANGELS CAN BE DOUCHEBAGS

29 October 2015

Over the last few weeks we have fallen behind in our work, and I thought some of you would be interested in the reasons why. One of the roles we, or rather I, have found myself in is being the default problem solver for some people in the esoteric community. Much of this is the result of a single article I wrote nearly twenty years ago on various forms of pathology that can occur on the spiritual journey. In recent years this increasingly included working not only with the common occurrence of "spiritual crises" but with individuals and families who have genuine psychic and spiritual toxicity dominating their lives. Recently I was asked by a well-known and successful fellow who is also a ceremonial magician if I could help out a friend of his who lived several hours from me. I listened to the story and it was straightforward: a magical operation went bad, and now the entire family was experiencing the weight of toxic strain it was creating.

The fellow who undertook the operation is also a well-known professional who has fallen on some hard times and wanted to "get his game back," so to speak. He was used to a high income and wanted it back, as he and his family had grown accustomed to it.

To do this he did not, as I initially expected, work with *goetic* demons, but instead called upon a planetary angel. Another well-known author had even provided him with extensive divinatory readings on the operation, and for a period of time afterward. Yet not only was the return to professional and financial success not realized, but serious and peculiar health issues developed. A general malaise began to fall over everyone in the house. Despite the promises of success in the divinatory readings—all of which I read—not a *single one* proved accurate in the least way. Financial, professional, and health problems mounted. Just when they were at the end of their rope they finally asked for help; as a result, I was called in.

I reviewed the situation in detail, spoke to all concerned, and even read all of the extensive journal entries regarding the events leading up to, during, and after the operation. With a plan in mind, I began to believe I knew what had happened, what had gone wrong.

You see, for every action there is an equal and opposite reaction, and in this case, the demonic or chaotic had managed to slip in. Dion Fortune wrote about it, Jean Dubuis mentioned it, and I have stated it many times: when we call upon the forces of angels or the Spheres, we also indirectly call upon the demonic or *qlipothic* as well. In fact, Dr. Rudd even clearly states that the chaotic will attempt to interrupt angelic operations, a fact that is often ignored and overlooked. Seeking to change something *means*, obviously, there is something that must be changed. That something is always first and foremost our own inherent qualities of inertia, selfishness, and habituated patterns.

As a result, for this fellow (and I am amazed at the errors that were made by those involved), the desire to get back to the way of life he and his family members were accustomed to living overruled his common sense, and that of his diviner as well. The obvious was ignored.

So, after much travel, work with the family, and personal preparation, we were able to clean things up and restore balance to the household and its members. However—and here is what is most important to you—what came to my attention was this: the so-called angels are the managers of the universe; asking them for help is like going to a sponsor and asking for a donation. The sponsor always asks, "Who benefits?" If they like your answer you get the money; if not, no money. So, how do we get a sponsor's money? We demonstrate a program of increased efficiency that has a positive impact on the widest possible group of beings. Simply put, you do not get money simply because you have a "great idea," but because when implemented, that idea helps more people than just those directly involved. In other words, the ripple effect. Who does this serve?

This fellow was going to help himself, his family, and through them a general broader audience, but there was no direct mention of anything for his lodge, church, or even business and those it employed. There was no goal other than to get a certain amount of money to work on a personal goal—a goal whose impact on anyone other than a small number of people was unclear. Was it a bad goal? Did it injure anyone? No. It was simply a very selfish one, in that "neutral-selfish" kind of way.

So, after spending hours working with the family in prayer and ritual, and then salting and burning all of the ritual para-phernalia involved, destroyed so that "not even their names or images remained," I was given a box containing several rare volumes of books, and then, like the main character Alex Bernier in the 2003 movie starring Heath Ledger, *The Order* (also released as *The Sin Eater*), I was told to take whatever I wished from the extensive collection of rare volumes. I pulled a few and did not abuse their generosity.

This also raises the question of psychic contamination, a key element of magic going back to its origins. Is it possible to be contaminated by ritual paraphernalia or even an envi-ronment? The answer is *yes*; that is why we must be careful in what we accept as gifts from others, where we work, and what we do there, as well as be sure to keep our own sense of positive regard and goodwill toward others at a strong level. Keeping the well-being of others in mind or, as my great-uncle used to say, being 51% altruistic (working for others without concern of reward), is a good way of keeping ourselves free from having operations go toxic, and ourselves along with them. But to do this, we need to truly understand our motives. We need to really understand the nature of our own mind.[1]

---

[1]To help you do this we have posted audio files on YouTube under the Institute for Hermetic Studies Channel, and we encourage you to listen to and apply their teachings.

GHOSTS AND STUPID THINGS PEOPLE DO

11 March 2016

During one of the afternoon sessions of our recent seminar, *Pathology of the Sublime*,[1] we spoke about some of the things people do when confronted with unpleasant paranormal experiences. These mostly involve what are lumped under the generic terms of "haunting" or "poltergeist activity." Regardless of how you may wish to dissect these terms or use others, the commonalities still apply: *people are stupid*.

Now, just to be clear I will repeat myself: *people are stupid*.

This stupidity, or dullness, manifests as an inability to think and act productively and is born of several causes— mainly fear. This is important, because fear encompasses a host of sub-issues, including the fact that humans are not *rational* beings but *emotional* ones AND that they are creatures of habit. Lump these together under the wrapping and ribbon of fear and you have the recipe for a slow-moving train wreck.

This train wreck also has some common landmarks along the way, the most important being the tendency for at least one or more of those involved to have an interest or belief in ghosts, demons, generic horror-movie stuff, etc., etc., but no real spiritual life. Now, this takes us to the important part: an interest in the paranormal, psychic phenomena, other planes of existence, and the host of invisible beings that may or

---

[1] Available on the IHS YouTube channel and as Volume VII of the IHS Study Guide Series.

may not coexist with us in and of itself does *not* constitute a spiritual study or a spiritual practice.

This is very important, as this is the basis for their fear: the feeling that they have no control over what is happening and are simply victims. It also means that even when they are given instructions on how to address the issues by themselves, in nearly every instance they do not. Even if they want to, they allow someone else in the living arrangement or their life to keep them from acting in a manner that will put an end to the disturbing phenomena.

This last part is critical, because this is what allows the situation to continue to deteriorate until, finally, there is no alternative but outside help (possibly of a dubious nature) or collapse into despair.

I bring this up because over the last few years we have seen in the publishing and broadcast industries a massive production of materials dealing with ghosts, hauntings, possession, and related "spooky" stuff. These are nearly always treated in a very sensational manner, giving a false impression of the cosmos and our place in it. Studying the paranormal devoid of a traditional initiatic system is tricky at best. Note I say *initiatic system* and not *religious*, as too many religious beliefs of a highly dualistic nature have crept into the means by which popular culture addresses these issues.

For those interested in the paranormal, we encourage you to study it in relation to or directly as part of the curriculum of an initiatic system. If this is not possible, then certain practices found in the book *Kabbalah for Health and Wellness*[2] and in the Institute for Hermetic Studies Audio Program on ritual purity and exorcism[3] will be of benefit to you.

---

[2] See the Second Revised & Expanded Edition, *op. cit.*

[3] Available on the Institute for Hermetic Studies YouTube channel.

THE PROBLEM OF EVIL

12 June 2004

The problem of evil is a perennial one for students of esotericism. Various philosophies address the problem in different manners, but in synthesis there seem to be several distinct areas of overlap and agreement.

While alchemy does not address the idea of evil directly, it speaks of purification, sublimation, and other acts suggesting that our emotions, physical matter, and thoughts can exist in an imperfect state and somehow be brought to perfection or, at the very least, to a more desirable condition. All matter is imperfect compared to the spiritual archetype that it incarnates, but it is *not* "evil" (that is, in active and conscious rebellion against the "Good").

Gnosticism addresses evil in two ways: relative and absolute. Matter and material life are seen as undesirable, as they are prison houses of the spirit. Like various schools of yoga and Buddhism, material life is to be escaped from and is *de facto* evil. Matter keeps us from being free, unhindered, spiritual beings without temptations or passions. This is interesting in light of the idea that the early angels united with "the daughters of men" and thereby created offspring of legend referred to as "giants" in the Old Testament. Clearly being "spiritual" or without a physical body isn't enough when it comes to being passionless, but this seems to escape most of the discussion in this area.

Kabbalah remains among the most balanced of approaches

in that it sees evil as relative and necessary. It is to be overcome without condemning the material world.

In fact, in Kabbalah and alchemy, material life *is* our life. It is where we are in the here and now. We can think of Earth as a school, a prison, a blank slate, or as whatever we like. Even if we believe in life having an evolutionary purpose and the influence of astrological Signs and Ages to push humanity along, life has no meaning until we *give it* meaning. All the guiding and directing in the cosmos is worthless unless we commit ourselves to a cause, something greater than ourselves, and work to express it, even if we may not live to see its fruition.

The great cathedrals of Europe, temples of the ancients, and other places of majesty and wonder were built by people who would never live to see them completed. While for many of them it was "just a job," same as any other (or forced labor as a slave or serf), many of the artisans and professional builders employed took great pride in their work and saw it for what it was: a monument to something greater than the limits of earthly human life. Even in anonymity, their lives had, and still do have, great meaning, as we worship, tour, or simply admire from a distance their labor, centuries after it was completed.

If you see material existence as good or evil, this is a reflection of your inner life. We hear often of the power of positive thinking, and the more cynical among us (who are often the more intelligent as well) sneer and either disregard it or simply pay lip service to the idea.

In truth, "Positive Thinking" is in many ways a lie. However, the reason is not in the idea, or theory, but in the *language used to transmit it*. When we conceptualize the idea of thinking, it is often relegated to the idea of problem solving and, as such, rational and logical processes. However, thinking is *more* than logic, or problem solving: it is our worldview. Our thinking is the filter we use to process the world, how it works, our place in it, and our relationship to others.

The greatest power in our thinking process is not our ability to reason and use logic, but our ability to *feel*. Our emotions are our greatest asset in this area. If we feel positively about life, then life takes on a flavor, color, or experience that logic and reason cannot transmit. Emotions are the driving force, the energy of the psyche, of human consciousness. When we talk of the "Power of Positive *Thinking*" what is really being referred to is the "Power of Positive *Feeling*."

Studies have shown that optimists are more successful than "realists." This fundamental fact explains why so many smart people are often so under-achieving, under-paid, and under-fulfilled in their lives.

Modern educational systems develop the rational and logical at the expense of the emotional. Cynicism is encouraged and rewarded by the media and academia. Yet if we look closely at "realists" we see that they are essentially looking for an excuse not to act. They are afraid of failure, of making a mistake, of essentially living, and also of dying.

If you come to accept your mortality, then fear drips away, and problems of success, failure, or even good and evil take on a more manageable perspective. Accept this: *you will die*, so *act*, and act as if it is today, for someday it *will* be.

This doesn't mean that we throw away our resources or ignore reason and logic but, instead, after consideration, we still pick something and dedicate ourselves to its realization.

If you would like to be successful and find meaning in your life, you must first decide what is the single thing you want to accomplish. What do you want to dedicate your limited and numbered human days to promoting, building, and embodying, even if you do not live to see its fruition?

Second, *turn off your television*. Get rid of cable, satellite TV, or whatever it is that you plug into that drains your life force.

Third, meet and collaborate with others who are seeking to build and promote their lives, even if their projects are not esoteric or spiritual in nature, so long as they are developing, encouraging, and demonstrating the effectiveness of an optimistic attitude.

Fourth, do not discuss your plans with anyone who cannot directly assist you in their fruition. Avoid nay-sayers and similar "realists" who will tell you from their position of superiority (built upon a mountain of failure and self-imposed fears and limitations) that, whatever "It" is, "It can't be done."

Fifth, read biographies about the great men and women who have overcome all obstacles to achieve their dreams. Even if the books are older, and the stories slightly romanticized, read them anyhow. It is inspiration and example that you are seeking to internalize and emulate, not a tell-all exposé. A wonderful example of this kind of inspirational biographical writing is *Twelve Against the Gods* by William Bolitho.[1]

Sixth, and finally, *give back*, here and now. Generosity is a form of confidence in the future, as well as gratitude for what you have. Give of your time, knowledge, and material wealth. All three must be given for this to work, because in doing so, you create a chain of events and habits that will cascade back to you and reward you with opportunities otherwise outside your reach. In your acts of generosity of time, talent, and treasure, your true inner attitude and deepest-held feelings are revealed. The time, however, is *now*, and without concern for any personal reward that might come as a result of your actions; give, give generously, give wisely, give regularly, and give impersonally.

In doing this, you create a better life for yourself, and a better world for others in which evil has no place to hide or to grow.

---

[1] William Bolitho, *Twelve Against the Gods: The Story of Adventure* (New York: Viking, 1962).

OUR
TRUE WILL

Your Happiness is the Only Thing That Really Matters

26 March 2016

In the circles of spirituality (and politics) we are often told that our happiness lies in others. While it is true that "no man (or woman, for that matter) is an island" it *is* a stretch to go from saying that our lives interact to saying that I am only happy when others are happy. Too often we miss the point of the interdependency or interaction between people, and jump to the idea that I as an individual cannot be happy unless others are happy too. Sadly, this is reinforced in a lot of rhetoric coming out of Tibetan Buddhist communities, wherein the ideal of the Bodhisattva (selfless servant to the Tibetan Buddhist cause) is drummed into the heads of students—who for the most part simply want to lead happier and more productive lives and NOT become drafted into the cause of the "Tibetan Buddhist Imperial Complex" (TBIC). And Tibetan Buddhism in exile is not alone in this conscription process, nor in using guilt as a means of getting people to serve their particular vision of the "greater good"—we see it in nearly every humanitarian, philanthropic, and spiritual enterprise that exists today.

Now, I get it, and I often speak and write about the importance of service. However, service must be of one's own "free will and accord," not out of social compulsion or guilt. Guilt is the feeling of inadequacy for not participating in the manner that is expected by others. When I attended Rhode

Island College (located in Providence) between 1989 and 1991 for my Master's Degree in Counseling, I had a wonderful teacher named Dr. Vincent Calia. Dr. Calia said, and I quote, "I don't do guilt. I either do something and enjoy it, or I don't do it." Now, being neither Catholic nor Jewish (two groups that make up the bulk of converts to Tibetan Buddhism in the West), I do not "do guilt" either. Needless to say, this creates a fair amount of consternation among many of the people I know who are on the spiritual path.

I encourage each of us to undertake introspection regarding our actions and their outcomes. I encourage each person to desire to be the best person he or she can be. But guilt is only one of the means we can use to begin the journey on the path of introspection; it is neither an end nor a good motivator for daily life. Guilt is toxic, and it can either direct us to a proper course of action where the poison becomes the cure, or it will grow stronger and kill us—slowly and painfully—but *unaddressed*, guilt will kill us for certain.

You see, your happiness is important. In fact, your happiness is the only thing that matters.

I know, many of you are gasping in anxiety as you read this, thinking, "What has gotten into him? How can he say such a selfish and self-centered thing? Doesn't he CARE that there is suffering in the world?" Now pause for the silent scream.

Okay, yeah, I know. Starving babies, terrorism, end of the world in some ecological catastrophe, yadda, yadda, yadda...

Now that we have that out of the way, so what? What can I or you do about it? For the most part, somewhere between little and nothing on any level large enough to make an immediate impact that will change the course of events. That is the hard, cold reality of it. Too many of you reading this are powerless in this world or in any other, and are easily manipulated by people who are smarter, more driven, and more successful than you are at the current moment.

Read that again, and let it sink in, because that is the

way it is and will continue to be unless you do one thing:

Realize and act upon the reality that the only thing you have any control over is your own mind and, with it, your happiness and your life. If you are happy, then that means you have successfully navigated through the white water of life, and can be a useful friend and guide to others. If you are happy, that means you can be a focal point of successful living—and *living* is your only purpose. You are not here to wait until you die, or to suffer through it: *you are here to live.*

Your *life* is your Path; it is your teacher. Your desires are your inner creative impulses coming from deep inside your mind into the world of action—of cause and effect, of matter. If you pay attention to those desires when they are fresh and act upon them, they can lead you to experiencing a great deal of joy and happiness in a manner that is free from guilt, clinging, fear, and grasping. If they are ignored, they become toxic, and over time become a poison that permeates your life and the lives of those around you. As a therapist, nearly every one of my clients suffered from life-threatening mental health and addiction issues because they were stunted at some point in their creative expression. Many were very successful in business, sports, and other activities, but there was always something that they wanted to do, did not, and it became a source of dissatisfaction for them that turned toxic through neglect. Toxic emotions are death. Unexpressed desires—and by that you know I mean desires wherein no harm is done to another—are the source of suffering in nearly everyone I have every met.

From wanting to write a novel, memoir, or song, to wanting to be an actress, singer, artist, pilot, or doctor, each of these unexpressed desires have been a source of suffering for the one who carried it—AND, by extension, for those around them.

I will say more about this at some point later, but for now, I want each of you to remember that your very being, your very "enlightenment," your very existence is based upon your unassailable and unique individuality. Spend some time with that. *You are responsible for you.* When you do that well, then you are able to be responsible toward others. If you can take care of your own life, then it is easier to trust in you that you can help others learn to take care of theirs. Your joy is not my joy, as I am free to accept it or reject it, as is your suffering. My enlightenment is not yours, although it can be a vehicle that helps in the process. If it were not this way then one enlightened being is all it would take and the rest of us would be enlightened by default.

Your individuality is unassailable, that is, it cannot be compromised by anything exterior to you. Once you accept this, and take responsibility and control for your individuality and mind, then happiness is nearly instantaneous. It also means that you no longer fear the world or what goes on in it. "Unassailable" means that you have self-confidence and, with it, the ability to solve problems as they arise before you. In doing so, your sphere of influence increases, and your ability to be of SERVICE and assistance to others increases naturally and WITHOUT EFFORT. There is no striving for sainthood, adeptship, or some marker of spiritual superiority. Instead, your daily life becomes your mark of rank, and your light radiates, because that is all it can do, for, as we are told, we cannot "hide our light under a bushel." This also means that there is no compulsion to join—or leave for that matter—any group, cause, movement, or organization to make a positive difference in the lives of others. Your daily activities will be your cause and your clients, customers, employees, and co-workers those you serve. You may also be inspired to affiliate with others, start a project or activity, and make or undertake a specific project. If so, wonderful. It will be spontaneous, from within, and therefore far more successful, as it will be fueled by joy rather than out of a sense of unwanted duty or a task you need to do and then "you can get on with your life."

Now spend some time with this and contemplate what it is you need to do to be happy. How will you undertake that activity? Contemplate your existence as an unassailable individual, and how you want to express that in your life. The more you can express yourself, the more you can do in your own life, and the more genuinely spontaneous you are all translates into the more you can do for helping other people improve their lives as well.

This is the true expression of spirituality, or enlightened action, and it all starts and ends with *you*.

OPTIMISM AND TERROR

THE REALITY OF DAILY LIFE

22 March 2016

I woke up this morning to an email and, like each of you, to news of the terrorist attacks in Brussels. The email asked me, "Mr. Stavish, in light of your optimistic can-do attitude, how does this play out against the world of current events?"

The answer is simple, but before I get to it, let me give you a little background.

Several days ago I had an intimation (I hesitate to call it a fully formed intuitive awareness, more like a strong hunch) that Brussels would experience a terrorist attack in two or three days. It did. This is not the first time I have had these kinds of insights, and some have been very specific— e.g., the morning of 9/11, the tsunami from the 2004 Indian earthquake, the assassination of Yitzhak Rabin in 1995. Each of the last three occurred to me on the morning of the event, long after the process was in motion, and there was nothing I could do about it. Let's face it, even if I did call the FBI or some such agency, other than get me on the "kook list," what would come from it?

So, what is a modest and unwitting clairvoyant to do?

Do your best, that is all you can do. That is all any of us can do, psychic or not.

Now, this is important, so pay attention.

If each of us is living to the best of our abilities, we become a focal point, a pinpoint of Light, Life, and Love for others. We become an example, and the ripple effect of taking care of ourselves, our families, and communities can reach out well beyond our physical locations. This is compounded when those we are around on a daily basis see us as examples and, in turn, create healthy, happy, and productive lives for themselves, their families, and their friends. The circles interact and expand, gaining momentum as they proceed.

Now, just as I had insight into the death and terror some people were about to unleash, maybe others—unknown to me—have an inkling of what I or others are doing and they are inspired or motivated to either do something creative or cease doing something criminal and destructive. Maybe, in some strange fashion, you or I when in prayer and meditation, appear to others as angels, saints, or some kind of spiritual being and it inspires or helps them. I do not know, but I am optimistic that it happens. If I can get a glimpse of the mind of a murderer unknown to me, who is thousands of miles away, then I am certain that someone in need who wants to be happy, healthy, and creative will get a glimpse of someone else's mind and be aided by it. That is the basis, after all, of the so-called "guru yoga" of Indian and Tibetan tantra and of Assumption of the Godform.

"Thoughts are things," we have been told, and this is why cynicism is so destructive to our progress on the Path. Cynicism starts as the negation of others, but in truth, it is the negation of ourselves. It is the eradication of our self-respect and self-confidence. In the words of Kabbalah, it is the "shell" of our being, and therefore the seeds of the demonic whose fruit can only be destruction, disease, and death instead of construction, health, and life.

Two days ago I posted an article on the importance of peak experiences, self-confidence, optimism, and self-expression. Yesterday I asked each of you to share it with one more person. I know that few of you did, and it is for this reason that I am asking each of you again to share it—to share it with as many people as you can. Make it go viral. Become part of the solution to your problems, those around you, and those you will never meet. Be confident, just as I am confident as I write and send this to you, that you can and are making a difference in your life and the world as a whole. Have the courage to stand up and be confident, to be a role model of optimism, creativity, and problem solving for others by consciously directing their minds (and thereby efforts) toward those goals. The more we think about peak experiences, the easier it is to have them. The more we have them, the more contagious they become. You may never know whose life you have changed for the better, but simply by being the best person you can be, you have had a positive effect on an untold number of people.

Now, again, I am asking each of you to share this essay with your friends, family, associates, and anyone you can. Not everyone will respond well to the message, but that is all right. This is not about convincing others; it is about laying the groundwork of ideas so that they may take root in the proper soil. In the end, you will have done all that you can, and that is all you can do. Be joyful in your efforts and in the fruits of your thoughts and actions.

Spring, Life, Peak Experiences, & Why Smart People Fail

(But Can Succeed as Well)

16 November 2016

As I sit here writing this note, astronomical Spring has arrived. It arrives every year, like clockwork, because it *is* clockwork, so to speak. Each year it comes and goes just as it has done since we started having something that resembles four seasons in the Northern Hemisphere in the distant past and started tracking it with the stars. It comes, it goes—and yet, no one expects it to be gone forever.

As I sit here I am reading a book that arrived a few days ago. It is *Superconsciousness: The Quest for the Peak Experience* by Colin Wilson.[1] He wrote it when he was seventy-five years of age as a distillation and "do-it-yourself manual" on the topic.

Now, this is important.

You see, esotericism, or at least a large part of it, is really all about having and utilizing peak experiences, so *anything* that gets us into a peak frame of mind is a good thing and supports in some way our personal and spiritual awareness. Anything that takes us away from peak experiences is counter-productive to our path or indicates something that we need

---

[1]Colin Wilson, *Superconsciousness: The Quest for the Peak Experience* (London: Watkins, 2009).

to be aware of and pay attention to so as to overcome it and get back into or onto the "peak."

In his Foreword, Wilson summarizes a theme that I have addressed in various ways for several years now. It is the notion of the cultural zeitgeist of the twentieth (and now twenty-first) century: that of a "defeat bias" or "you can't win" attitude in popular culture—and therefore in the mass consciousness of people. Wilson calls this the "fallacy of insignificance": the idea that life is one long drawn-out defeat.

Both Wilson and Abraham Maslow, founder of the modern theory of peak experiences, discussed this and its implications at length. Maslow found that when he discussed peak experiences with his students *they felt better*. They accessed more of themselves, performed better, and were happier, successful, and optimistic. This feedback loop continued and had actual concrete effects on their lives. The inverse of this is that when people complain, focus on negative outcomes (rather than problem solving and solutions), and past defeats, they become depressed (anger expressed inwardly), aggressive (anger expressed outwardly), and life then becomes a meaningless experience. Disease, self-destruction, and death follow in its wake.

Over the decades I have had the opportunity to know many people, most of them well-educated. What makes the successful ones different from those who are not successful is very often the ability to adapt to circumstances (we call that evolution) and optimism (a positive view of the future or the outcomes of their actions), united by self-confidence (a healthy self-image). Now, some of you will dismiss this as self-serving pop-sales psychology, but it is not. It is the foundational basis of all occult practices, as well as of yoga, Vajrayāna Buddhism, and anything of value that requires us to get out of bed in the morning.

On the other hand, I have met many highly educated individuals who keep telling me how the world works, and yet—despite their myriad academic degrees, honors, publications, or membership in high IQ societies—their overall accomplishments are relatively nominal. Above all, they are not very happy.

The reason? *They recognize problems, but not solutions—* or at least not solutions that actively involve their time, talent, and treasure. They are good at saying what others should or ought to do, but stop short of doing anything themselves (at least on a sustained level) that involves themselves as the active player. They also share a common habit: they complain, criticize, and point out the actual or perceived failings of others without pointing out anything good that the other party may be doing. Instead of building something for themselves and others, they spend their time attempting to cut others down.

I see and read this a lot in contemporary occultism: authors telling us of great possibilities who in their own lives are barely able to pay the light bill. Now, we all have ups and downs in life. We all experiences highs (or peaks if you will) and the depths of despair. Learning to navigate these extremes is a function of any worthwhile life philosophy. What I am talking about, however, is something different. What I am talking about is a basic failure to let the negative go, focus on the positive, and find solutions that start and maybe even end with yourself as the source of your own suffering and the solution to its elimination.

You see, your life is the only thing you are ultimately responsible for, and your attitude and self-concept the only things you can really control. When you are able to adapt to circumstances it means that you are relaxed and flexible, one of the key expressions of the enlightened state. When you are optimistic you are also expressing another foundational state of enlightenment and, when you are self-confident, you are expressing a foundational state of the enlightened mind: the basic nature of our very Self. These things combined form the holy trinity of what an enlightened being is like. If we want to be enlightened, then we need to act in accordance with our ideal. For this we have several methods, of which Assumption of the Godform is the most common. However, without the inner confidence that enlivens the practice, it is little more than fantasy or a dead visualization. The same applies to any other ritual or practice we may undertake. It all begins and ends with *us* and our heartfelt self-image and how we nurture it daily.

So, for this year, I would like each of you to think, feel, and act *only from a state of adaptability, optimism, and self-confidence,* to remove limiting self-concepts from your thinking, speaking, and writing. If they must be expressed, do so in a manner that couples them to a solution or means of using them as a benchmark for progress and unfoldment. Sarcasm, cynicism, competitive comparisons, and general criticisms are to be wholly and completely eliminated. If this means completely eliminating all media input from television, movies, music, and maintaining silence in the company of friends and colleagues, then so be it.

In addition, I want each of you to focus on those things you did *well* and on the positive feelings it brought you. Speak about this with others. Make it the focal point of your interactions and weave it into any professional or group work you are doing. Get others, when possible, to focus on their peak experiences as well and see how it adds to the success of the endeavor. Remind yourself as often as possible of those "peak" times and rest in the joyful experience of the memory. Carry it forward, and let it carry you.

Each night, as the old Pythagoreans did, reflect and take stock of your day. Acknowledge your successes and act accordingly.

Sounds easy, right? Great! That means that by this time next year, each of you will be sending me an email of your experiences and progress. I look forward to hearing from you.

THE THIRD WAY

30 July 2016

Despite calls to "vote for the lesser of two evils" this November in the election for President of the United States, there is a third option that has not been widely discussed among those who would call themselves members of the "household of the faithful." This option is *renunciation.* You see, you are under no obligation to support one or the other of the two anointed candidates if your conscience says otherwise. You can in fact *not participate at all.* You do not have to vote. Now, it has been said in the past "don't complain if you don't vote"; however, that dates to a time when it was not so blatantly clear that (for at least one of the major parties) your opinion really does not matter. The corruption is widespread and blatant, and yet the true believers show their true colors (or rather, their true faith) by rallying around one of the two major candidates and then spewing vitriol upon those who do not wish to play that game.

There is a third option.

This option requires *real* faith, *real* courage, the genuine "bodhicitta" or "awakened heart-mind of enlightenment to spontaneous action," and not simply the mindless platitude of "compassion." This option requires a true "heart unafraid." Do not vote for a candidate you do not support. Do not vote out of fear. Vote for what you support, or do not vote at all.

But remember this...

Do it with *courage*—courage, faith, and confidence in yourself and your God or Gods. Do it with the knowledge that your Holy Guardian Angel is always with you and that you can and will deal with whatever life, the Fates, or your karma places before you. Act with genuine renunciation or unconcern for the outcome, because you believe in yourself and in your God, your karma, your Fate, Destiny, or whatever it is that guides and unfolds before you as an act of your own creation.

This path is a difficult one; it is easier to cling to one of the side pillars than to take the straight and narrow path up the center. It is easier to not act and condemn those who do, but that is not renunciation, that is arrogance and fear. Remember the words of Israel Regardie in his book *The One Year Manual*:

> NOW THAT, THROUGH THE pursuit of this series of psycho-spiritual disciplines, some degree of God-realization has been achieved...the student is faced by a most important decision. He is obliged to eradicate every vestige of duality from his thinking. Residues will cling to his mind, in very subtle ways. There is no God *and* the World—there is not God and himself. There is *only* God. All is God. Every trivial action is God-directed. Every single object in his environment is God endowed. Even the ego—though that seems to be the major obstacle to be gotten rid of—is God-determined. Yet he is a man or woman living for the moment in what appears to be a material world. He has to accept the world of appearances, the phenomenal world, exactly as it is...heat burns, cold freezes, [etc.]. Although each and every one of these phenomena are divine phenomena—and in their constant change are nonetheless representative of the ceaseless activity of the unchanging, omnipotent body of God—yet he must learn to keep all these diverse phenomena in their own place...

What then shall he do...to work His Will, to achieve other of his goals? ...He is surrounded by [people who] are hysterical, anxious, compulsive, disturbed by one event or problem after another, are sick and lame and halt. All this because they know not what or who they truly are.

How shall we presume to make them aware of their true nature without invading their precious privacy?

In other words, though he knows his own personal relationship to God... He must consider those methods whereby his needs are to be met that the divine purpose may be fulfilled.

There are many ways, of course, to do this. One of these is the method described in... *The Art of True Healing.* It is a method of mobilizing the spiritual power of the cosmos through the agency of Will, color, imagination and sound in order to achieve that which is required. It is an extension of the Middle Pillar where divine energy is concentrated and directed for specific use. ...There is another approach which is possible only to that student who has persevered with his own disciplines so that he has become an avenue through which the Divine Will may operate. Its outstanding merit is that it is simple and direct. It is not dissimilar to the classical religious one of accepting Jesus as one's personal Lord and Savior, and turning one's life over to Him. This approach has it that we are eager to find Him when we come to realize that there is no source of power in ourselves, that we are wholly dependent on Him. We become eager to connect up with this Source of Life and Power when we know that it makes wisdom, power and love available for us. It is "the strait gate," "the narrow way," and "few there be that find it." ...In this work...we use the term "The Holy Guardian Angel" as the term for our own Higher Self. He is an angel, mighty and powerful and is our own personal link with the universal God, and so it is to Him that we submit ourselves for the fulfillment of His Will, which at the same time, and paradoxically, is our will.

We cannot make a vital contact with our Angel by goodness or obedience...

Nor may we find him because of our good deeds. At best, our good deeds are only the evidence that we have found him... Nor do we find Him by a belief in any religious, metaphysical or occult doctrine. At best these are intellectual constructs for the expansion of our minds, but later come to have profound meaning as useful constructs only after we have found Him.

If we are willing to persevere, to be patient, and to work at self-discipline, to aspire and to invoke often, the Angel will enable us to do all of this.

...We do not have to do violence to ourselves to force ourselves to believe in Him; there is no need for force. We do *not have to will ourselves to believe. We need only to be willing*, [emphasis added] to make the necessary set of gestures, sincerely and honestly—and then *work and invoke often!*

It entails trusting the Holy Guardian Angel with all areas of our lives. In this we must face our egotism to realize that of ourselves we can do nothing, and what we are able to do can only result in futility and frustration. It means trusting the Angel to renew our character; we cannot do it ourselves. We turn over to Him the entire psyche, with all its conscious and unconscious problems and complexes which we have become acquainted with through the agency of the former exercises—and perhaps through some psychotherapeutic work. But we leave it to Him to clean out the filth from the stables—when it ceases to be filth. Only He can do it; of ourselves we are impotent.

It means allowing Him to dictate all our activities and keeping our hands and minds from meddling with His work, reserving them only as tools which He can use as He sees fit for our betterment and progress. We must not interfere with what He has to do.

It means trusting Him as to our health and financial security. This does not mean that we become careless of our nutritional intake, our clothes or personal hygiene, or that we drive the automobile with eyes closed. But it does mean that we stop worrying about what is going to become of us. We do the very best we can in any situation, knowing that He is guiding and guarding us... It means laying aside all our petty ambitions and objectives and permitting Him to plan our life for us. It may not result in the fulfillment of every ambition and objective, but we learn to rely solely upon Him, knowing that we will be guided constantly and continuously whether we are aware of it or not. It means putting away all our nice little occult philosophies and systems where everything is put into a neat cubbyhole and neatly compartmentalized and letting Him lead us to the Truth. It is the joy of putting aside our human frailties, of allowing Him to sanctify us...

...This is the magical way, of letting the Angel do His work among the living, of having placed oneself under the ægis of the Angel after having worked and prayed and invoked. From now on, the responsibility for all one's life in all its phases is taken from our petty ego with its limited vision and scope, and its wretched lust for results, and surrendered gladly to this higher agency which is *Oneself Made Perfect...*

> *I am He, the bornless Spirit, having sight in the feet, strong, and the immortal Fire.*
> *I am He, the Truth.*
> *I am He, who hate that evil should be wrought in the world.*
> *I am He, that lighteneth and thundereth.*
> *I am He, from whom is the shower of the Life of Earth.*

I am He, whose mouth ever flameth.
I am He, the begetter and manifestor unto
    the Light.
I am He, the Grace of the World.
"The Heart Girt with a Serpent" is my
    name.[1]

In his book *Vectors of the Counter-Initiation*, Charles Upton puts the current situation in these terms:

> The Desert Fathers and the Taoist Sages and the Sannyasins and the early Sufis knew quite well what was going on in the respective societies of their times; that's why they elected to leave those societies behind, either internally, through detachment and *apatheia* ["without suffering"—to not be disturbed by passions], or externally as well, by heading for the hills. Their *raison d'être*, like that of every true renunciate, is succinctly expressed in the following lines from the *Ramayana*:
>
>> In the first age of the world men crossed the ocean of existence by their spirit alone.
>> In the second age sacrifice and rituals began, and then Rama lived, and by giving their every action to him men lived well their ways.
>> Now in our age what is there to do but worship Rama's feet?
>> But, my friend, the last age of this world shall be the best, for then no act has any worth, all is useless...except only to say RAMA.[2]
>> The future will read this. Therefore, I tell them:

---

[1]Cf. Israel Regardie, *Twelve Steps to Spiritual Enlightenment* (Dallas, TX: Sangreal Foundation, 1969) 83-90.

[2]See: Mark Stavish, *How to Develop Your Psychic Powers* (IHS Monograph Series # 4: CreateSpace, 2016), for more information on the use of "Rama" and other mantras.

> When all is in ruin around you, just say Rama.
> We have gone from the spiritual to the
> passionate. Next will come Ignorance. Uni-
> versal war.
> Say Rama and win! Your time cannot touch
> you.

The "first age" in the Hindu conception is the age of sattva, of Knowledge; its appropriate spiritual Way is jñana-yoga. The "second age" is the age of rajas, of Passion; its appropriate Way is karma-yoga. The last age is the age of tamas, of Ignorance; its appropriate Way is bhakti-yoga. All three of these margas or sacred paths are possible in every age, as Ramana Maharshi...demonstrated. But our times are darker than his were. The one called to walk the path of jñana in these final days of the Kali-yuga may also be called, as we have said above, to understand This World, *al-Dunya* [the temporal world], as an engineered control system, especially as he or she—like almost everyone—has become involved with it; the ones who are born and remain innocent of world-liness are few and far between. In these times, to become conscious of how we are being controlled and terrorized is, precisely, to deconstruct the ego, or the greater part of it. It is to vomit out the World, to undergo the *catharsis* posited by the Greek tragedians, to "die before you die"... And, sometimes, the world just leaves you; this indicates that God, who is a jealous God, wants you for Himself.[3]

The choice—at the ballot box or otherwise—is always up to you. Relax, and choose wisely.

---

[3]Charles Upton, *Vectors of the Counter-Initiation: The Course and Destiny of Inverted Spirituality* (San Rafael, CA: Sophia Perennis, 2012) 330-32.

Leaving the Path

7 August 2016

As a young member in several esoteric orders I often wondered how people could belong to something for twenty or more years and then simply leave. How is it that they could drop membership, but also any or all relations, or even appear to abandon spirituality altogether? In those days of bright-eyed idealism it was easy to confuse the work of spirituality with the vehicle of teachings, and in some instances, even the people who provided them. Such confusion is not uncommon, but also encouraged in many circumstances.

I am sure that each of you reading this has asked yourself the same or similar questions, and maybe you have even come to some of the same conclusions that I will outline. In *Light on the Path: A Study Guide for Qabala, Alchemy & Astrology*,[1] some guidelines were provided for those running or wishing to run a study group or formal lodge. The primary focus of those guidelines can be understood with the following statements:

- Spiritual practice must encourage personal responsibility.

- Spiritual practice must encourage healthy interpersonal relationships.

---

[1]Mark Stavish, *Light on the Path: A Study Guide for Qabala, Alchemy & Astrology* (IHS Study Guide Vol. I, 2014).

- Spiritual practice must build upon the previous two points and encourage independence and autonomy.

It is clear from many of the experiences each of us has had on the Path of Return—particularly when we walk it with others formally as "Brothers" and "Sisters" or informally— that unless the first two points are achieved, the third (that of autonomy) cannot be fully realized. True autonomy is not leaving your order or group in a snit, or waging flame wars against it or others. True autonomy is accepting things for what they are and recognizing your role in them, and what you want to and can do about it—if anything. Separation is often a part of autonomy, as the group mind of an organization or movement may force you out if you are not in a high degree of conformity with it. However, how we respond to this new direction is a matter of how well we have mastered the first two points of personal responsibility and healthy relationships. This is why in the guidelines in *Light on the Path* we actually encourage creating distance between oneself and one's group after a period of seven to twelve years. This starts with taking on less responsibility and concludes with an actual year off or "sabbatical" to relax and regroup before returning.

If you are wondering what kind of influence your esoteric practices may have on you, influences that are actually detrimental to your achieving personal responsibility and goals (the reason you started the Path to begin with), and healthy relationships with those outside of the group or movements, try this for forty days. Remove all reminders of your spiritual practice from visible daily sight. Place them in storage, or if you have a private chamber or oratory, leave everything there, but strip it to bare minimum. Place all initiation certificates, images, charters, special robes, etc., into boxes, and leave nothing esoteric visible in the common areas of your dwelling—box your books as well.

Then notice what your mind gravitates toward. What

areas of your life have you left undone? These will be the areas of your life that you need to apply your attention to so that you may better express your SELF as an autonomous being.

After forty days bring everything back out and pay attention to your feelings and responses to the collection of artifacts. Now, please be clear. During this time you may continue your periods of self-reflection, meditation, and inner work. Simply notice what and how it changes when you truly open up the mystery that is your SELF, rather than the Lesser or Greater Mysteries of this or that tradition, order, lodge, or group. This will help a great deal in understanding the immense power of the group mind as well as the power of suggestion.

Sometimes leaving the Path for a little while is the best way we can come to realize just how well we have mastered it and applied it to our daily life, or if it has mastered us and made us a servant of the dream.

THOSE WHO KNOW ARE SILENT

10 March 2008

Holy art Thou, who by thy Word has constructed all
that is; Holy art Thou, whose brightness, nature has
not darkened; Holy art Thou, of whom all Nature
is an image... Accept pure offerings of speech from
a soul and heart uplifted to thee, Thou of whom
no words can tell, no tongue can speak, whom only
silence can express.[1]

> — From Book One of the *Hermetica*,
> attributed to Hermes the Thrice Great

Lama Govinda (1898-1985), a German veteran of the First
World War, ex-patriot, and pioneer of bringing Tibetan Buddhism to the West, wrote two landmark books which remain
classics generations after first appearing in print: *Foundations
of Tibetan Mysticism*[2] and *The Way of the White Clouds*.[3]
Foundations addresses the underlying psychology of Tibetan
Buddhist practices, as well as its emphasis on the power of
sound, or mantra, in the process of achieving Enlightenment,

---

[1]Cf. Clement Salaman, et al., *op. cit.*, 24.

[2]Anagarika Govinda, *Foundations of Tibetan Mysticism: According
to the Esoteric Teachings of the Great Mantra, Oṁ Mani Padme Hūṁ*
(London: Rider, 1959). Original text in German.

[3]Anagarika Govinda, *The Way of the White Clouds: A Buddhist
Pilgrim in Tibet* (London: Hutchinson, 1966).

or Illumination. In a compilation by Richard Power of several of Govinda's lesser-known essays, *The Lost Teachings of Lama Govinda*,[4] our German Tibetophile demonstrates many similarities between the writings of the French Jesuit and scientist Teilhard de Chardin and Buddhist philosophy. While it is not known to what degree either man was familiar with Hermetic philosophy, it is also clear that their statements are in sympathy with it.

Tibetans are taught to view all of matter as an expression of cosmic order, and enlightenment as a different phase of becoming. As modern kabbalists like to say, "Kether is in Malkuth and Malkuth is in Kether, except of a different nature." More clearly, it is stated in the Heart Sutra: "form is emptiness, and emptiness is form." For de Chardin in his work *Hymn of the Universe*, we see these insights expressed:

> I bless you matter, and you I acclaim; not as the pontiffs of science and moralizing preachers depict you, debased, disfigured—a mass of brute forces and base appetites—but as you reveal yourself to me today, in your totality and your true nature... The aspect of life which most stirs my soul is the ability to share in an undertaking, in a reality, more enduring than myself; it is in this spirit and with this purpose in view that I try to perfect myself and master things a little more. When death lays its hand upon me it will leave intact these things, these ideas, these realities which are more solid and precious than I... What I want my God, is that by a reversal of my forces (of consciousness) which you alone can bring about, my terror in the face of the nameless changes destined to renew my being be turned into an overflowing joy at being transformed into you.[5]

---

[4] Richard Power, *The Lost Teachings of Lama Govinda: Living Wisdom from a Modern Tibetan Master* (New Delhi: New Age Books, 2009).

[5] Pierre Teilhard de Chardin, *Hymn of the Universe* (New York: Harper & Row, 1961) 66-67.

The inward-turning of our consciousness—not in a rejection of matter, but to better understand it by penetrating into its deepest secrets—is the essential technique of alchemical meditation, tantric exercises, and the insightful process of de Chardin—a form of Jñana Yoga if you will, through a contemplative form of study founded upon a correct view of Being or the mind.

In fact, de Chardin states that we only become *spiritual* when we become *creative*. That is, we make choices, understand cause and effect, the fruits of our actions, and in doing so, become conscious. We become awake or illumined in slow and progressive degrees. This understanding of our self as a mirror image of God, or as microcosm, ultimately gives understanding of the macrocosm as a natural aspect of inner unfoldment. Or as the ancient aphorism of the Greek Mysteries, those descended from the land of Khem, state it, "Know thyself, and you will know the gods."

The most common trait among those who have had this insight, this opening of their inner eye into the reality of their own being, their own mind, and its mirror of the Cosmos, is that most often *they are silent about it*. Jesus spoke of the Kingdom of Heaven being within or among us and taught us to pray, "Thy Kingdom come, Thy will be done, on Earth as it is in Heaven."[6] Metaphysical abstractions are absent from the skeletal and fragmentary record we have of his teachings. Jesus was pragmatic in his method and doctrines. Siddhartha never spoke of God or cosmic realities and focused only on helping each person understand their own mind that they may understand the nature and source of suffering and liberation. The Hermetic teachings are filled with cosmic notions that in the end are used to demonstrate that there is no difference between the mind of man and the mind of God, and that all apparent notions of "material" and "spiritual" are mental constructs. "As above, so below; as below, so

---

[6]Matthew 6:10.

above. To accomplish the miracle of the One Thing."[7]
Lama Govinda states,

> The silence of the Buddha was more significant than
> all our words. It was the silence of the ultimate in-
> expressible mystery that is open to all, but which
> must be approached by each single person alone. It
> is the mystery of that center all human beings share,
> in which the whole universe is contained. This center
> is all-comprehensive depth consciousness, in which
> the sum total of all experiences and all forms of life
> of the beginningless and endless circle of all events of
> the universe is accumulated. It is called in Buddhist
> terminology "the treasure house of consciousness"
> (*alaya-vijnana*), and in this center the solidarity of
> all beings is contained. It is the source of all creative
> forces. Without reaching this center, we cannot find
> liberation. But because this center contains the soli-
> darity of all living beings, we cannot liberate ourselves
> without sharing this liberation with all humanity, as
> I think Christ has already demonstrated. The light
> of God would be what in Buddhism we call "the
> consciousness of enlightenment" (*bodhicitta*), which
> consists of becoming conscious individually of that
> universal center within us.[8]

Awakening to this individual consciousness of the universal
center within has at times been assisted by various forms of
ritual initiation, almost always of a dramatic and extremely
traumatic nature. It is no surprise that it is also associated
with extreme illness, accidents, and near-death experiences
as well, while almost universally occurring suddenly and
unexpectedly. Yet this awakening is just that, an awakening
or insight into the totality of reality. It is not a permanent
state of consciousness. It is a crack in the door of our psyche,

---

[7]The Emerald Tablet of Hermes.

[8]Richard Power, *The Lost Teachings of Lama Govinda, op. cit.*,
50-51.

not a full opening and entering into the room of our Being. Those who can enter at will we call adepts; those who live there, we call masters, saints, Enlightened Beings.

The gradual understanding of ourselves, our very mind or consciousness, how it functions, and what it is, is the measure of our unfoldment, our adepthood. The more we unfold the more we become both an individual and aware of the whole. We do not become "a part of the whole" in that we merge our mind with the cosmic mind into the great sleep of Hindu nirvana, but we are instead fully aware of our essential unity with all, and of the effects of our actions on our self as well as others, physical and non-physical. This is awakening to the Law of Cause and Result—the only law that truly rules our life and all of creation.

MY
TEACHERS

Sometime in the spring—May, I believe—of 1987, at the age of twenty-three, I was visiting Dr. Meera Sharma at her home near Lake Scranton. Dr. Sharma was a physician specializing in internal medicine who was very publicly active in the local Rosicrucian body, the Wilkes-Barre Pronaos. For about half of its fourteen-year existence, the Pronaos even met in the waiting room area of her office on the fifth floor of the Bank Towers Building in downtown Scranton. George Seman, also an active member and founder of the affiliated body several years earlier (1984), was also present; as such, it was little surprise to me when the two later married. At that time, her spacious and Indian-accented living room had become a veritable salon where it was possible to meet all sorts of wonderful people at any given time.

On this occasion, her father and mother were visiting from Bombay. "Sharma," as he preferred to be called, was a self-made man, having moved from Burma to Bombay some time in his youth (although I am not certain if it was before or during the Second World War). He eventually made his fortune after much hard work by designing a battery casing that could withstand the brutal Indian humidity. In addition, having begun his practice at the age of forty, he was a profound clairvoyant, and was frequently sought out at home in

Bombay and in Scranton for his advice. Also visiting that day
was a professor from East Stroudsburg University, Professor
Peter Roche de Coppens, tenured professor of Psychology
and Sociology.

Peter was a tall, fit, middle-aged man, just shy of fifty,
with a swath of hair pulled across his clearly balding head—
on him, however, it did not look bad. He was congenial and
smiling; in fact, when one met him he was *always* smiling, but
it was as I would later come to believe, not because he was
happy, but more because (I believe) he was performing. He
portrayed his life as magical, spontaneous, and wonderful all
of the time—even when confronted with obstacles. He spoke
of love and its various manifestations—he was like Anthony
Robbins and Leo Buscaglia combined.

Before leaving, we went for a walk down toward Lake
Scranton, a favorite destination of everyone who would visit
Meera, and upon returning he went to the trunk of his car
and pulled out a copy of his most recent book, *The Invisible
Temple: The Nature and Use of the Group Mind for Spiritual
Attainment*.[1] He inscribed in French the following: "Learn
French to accomplish the Great Work." He followed it with:
"Find the woman," meaning, to find a woman that inspires you
to greatness—the French version of the "dakhini principle,"
if you will. (I have succeeded at one, if not at the other!)

The fact that Manly P. Hall was looking for a replacement
to head the Philosophical Research Society was mentioned
to me; that is, Hall was looking for someone to groom. The
implication was that I should pursue that line of inquiry,
although no means of introduction was suggested or supplied.
Art Kunkin (whom I would not meet until seven years later)
was part of the PRS Board of Directors after the time of
Hall's death[2] Like nearly every organization, esoteric and

---

[1]Peter Roche de Coppens, *The Invisible Temple: The Nature and
Use of the Group Mind for Spiritual Attainment*, Llewellyn's Spiritual
Science Series (St. Paul, MN: Llewellyn, 1987).

[2]See the article in this collection: "Some Passing Thoughts on Dr.

mundane, built upon the foundation of a charismatic creator and leader, PRS nearly imploded with his death.[3]

After our meeting I read two of de Coppens's other books, *Apocalypse Now: The Challenges of Our Times*,[4] a semi-autobiographical work, and *The Nature and Use of Ritual for Spiritual Attainment: Great Christian Documents and Traditional Blueprints for Human and Spiritual Growth*.[5] The latter was more to my liking as it addressed the key Christian documents from an esoteric perspective while linking their ideas to the spheres of the Tree of Life. This was the first time I had heard of this idea, and I was entranced by it. I later would learn that other schools had used it, but along with the collapse of Christian tradition, there was also the collapse of Christian esotericism. The two, as we shall see, go hand in hand—but that story is for another time.

He was a Roman Catholic, a member of his local parish, and my wife Andrea and I even attended an Easter service with him. Afterward we returned to his house for a light repast of fruit and tea. When addressing the altar he bent forward, nearly level with the floor, so that the top of his head was pointed at the altar. This, he said, was to allow the energy to enter into his central channel or Middle Pillar. This is also a very old and traditional manner of approaching the altar. It is not surprising that in his later years he wrote mostly about Christian spirituality rather than directly addressing esotericism.

Joseph C. Lisiewski."

[3]For a critical look at Hall and PRS at this time see his biography *Master of the Mysteries: The Life of Manly Palmer Hall* by Louis Sahagun (Los Angeles: Process, 2008).

[4]Peter Roche de Coppens, *Apocalypse Now: The Challenges of Our Times*, Llewellyn's Spiritual Science Series (St. Paul, MN: Llewellyn, 1995).

[5]Peter Roche de Coppens, *The Nature and Use of Ritual for Spiritual Attainment: Great Christian Documents and Traditional Blueprints for Human and Spiritual Growth* (Washington, D.C.: University Press of America, 1977).

Peter was also an admirer of Padre Pio, the Italian stig-
matic, and stated to me that Pio had the ability to be understood in whatever language the listener spoke. While I have
not researched this to see if it is reported elsewhere, it is an
insight into de Coppens's life: he was a collector of people,
and of experiences with them—something I enjoy doing as
well, although to a more limited and more intimate extent.

He spoke vaguely of his involvement in various esoteric
movements, never really pinning anything down or disclos-
ing any of the details. He disliked the Rosicrucian Order
(AMORC), yet had no problem mentioning his having been
"invited to assist them [the French Grand Lodge] with a
project," and something similar with Raymond Bernard's
CIRCES (Knights Templar) organization, while stating that
he had been involved with the Societas Rosicruciana in America (SRIA) established by Dr. George Winslow Plummer.

His calling card read "Knights of Malta Consultant." The
website for The Knights of Malta states:

> The knighthood nature explains and justifies the
> maintenance of the noble nature of the Order, as
> most of its Religious Knights came from chivalrous
> and noble Christian families. Today the majority of
> Knights of Malta belong to all classes of society. The
> members of the Order may be defined as Catholics
> enlivened by altruistic nobleness of spirit and behav-
> ior. All Knights of Malta must meet the traditional
> requirement for the bestowing of knighthood: distin-
> guish themselves for special virtues. The knighthood
> nature of the Order has kept its moral value, charac-
> terized by the spirit of service, sacrifice, and discipline
> of today's Knights of Malta. Battles are no longer
> fought with swords, but with the peaceful tools of the
> fight against disease, poverty, social isolation, and
> intolerance, as well as witnessing and protecting the
> faith.

Once, as he sat to the left of me on a couch, arm outstretched in my direction, and laughed off the suggestion that Cagliostro might have been a legitimate adept—even a member of the Knights of Malta—asserting that "he would never be allowed in; they would not have him."

Yet for all this talk of groups, he never invited us to participate in any group activity. He mentioned having established groups, and groups using his works, but that was the total of it—nothing specific and substantial. It was all ideas. He loved ideas and was in love with the idea of being important and influential in world-shaping events. He let it be known that he traveled on three or four passports: Swiss, American, Italian, and Argentinian, I believe. Consciously or not, he projected the image of being a "secret agent man." The United Nations was mentioned several times, along with other hints of intrigue and special knowledge. One friend, who came to give a presentation and afterward spent the evening in the "salon" remarked about de Coppens: "He does not want to be the man on the throne, he wants to be the man who stands behind him and whispers in his ear."

During the walk after our first meeting, de Coppens told me, as we walked the last few yards back to Meera's house, "I am an elitist," meaning he believed that each person must achieve according to their own efforts and merits—that there was a distinct hierarchy to life, even if not seen or understood by others. He was (and at the time I was unfamiliar with the ideas) clearly an advocate of the Traditionalist school of thought, at least in part. At other times Peter also mentioned a quote from Nietzsche, and another I thought was from Goethe's *Faust* but which I have not identified. I remember them well: "Neither God nor the Devil respect a lazy man," and "Human, all too human."[6]

The first supports the notion of elitism, the second the reality of our condition: vanity, pride, lust, avarice, and a host of human vices continually attack us as we attempt to

---

[6]The English rendering of Friedrich Nietzsche's *Menschliches, Allzumenschliches: Ein Buch für Freie Geister* (Chemnitz, 1878).

better ourselves and the world.

Oddly, it would be easy to compare Peter to Joseph Lisiewski. On first glance, they are polar opposites. Dr. Lisiewski was born into a working-class family in the hard-coal, hard-drinking region of Pennsylvania and did all he could do financially to get through college. Dr. de Coppens was Swiss by birth, received his education at prestigious universities on scholarship, including a Woodrow Wilson Scholarship, and became a liberal arts professor. Yet, both were adamant about the correctness of their views, almost to the exclusion of all else. This I believe is the Vice of Pride raising its head, as these two very accomplished men approached even more deeply into the mysteries that lie behind the Veil, in what kabbalists call the heart of Tiphareth. The accomplishments of both men demonstrate the ability to make some level of conscious contact with all of the elements of the Tree of Life and to bring them through—to move them from being abstractions into full manifestations, be they literary or scientific.

However, both were, or are, genuine adepts in their own right, accomplished in both the mundane and metaphysical domains. Both men proclaimed a philosophy of elitism, and of a natural spiritual hierarchy, believing that one must first accomplish something worthwhile in this world, and be able to act with decisiveness and power. This last part is a key theme in Psychosynthesis, which both men applied diligently. Assiah is the World of Action. Karma is "action and result." You must be a "somebody" before you can approach the Nothingness. A strong and healthy ego that was capable of acting and achieving in the material world is the basis for spiritual activity—as well as the result of it. Both men were generous in their own ways, yet had little use for what we think of as the widespread, cradle-to-the-grave, modern public welfare state and, in fact, saw it as detrimental to the very people its advocates claim it helps.

Where Lisiewski's main concern in his writings and personal contacts was "results"—physical and material (the

Earth Element, if you will)—and how that relates to the unfoldment of the individual, de Coppens—coming from a place of greater financial security and class status—was concerned with the "ideas," the Air Element, and their effects on the unfoldment of the individual. Lisiewski and de Coppens based their teachings on the fundamentals of Christian theology and then, like Traditionalists, worked their esotericism and occultism from there. Both men in their writings and spiritual practices sought to demonstrate methods wherein individuals could become effective, healthy, and independent, and from that place work with and assist others in their Becoming on the Path of Return. While de Coppens spoke often of love, and defined it as "right relationships," he also stated that each of us must be able to "bring something to the table" of the relationship and not be dependent on others. Each is a pillar that supports the canopy that covers all parties involved.

It may even be possible to sum up de Coppens's philosophical view with the inscription he wrote when he presented Andrea, who was just beginning her doctoral program in Molecular Biology at Brown University on a full fellowship, with a copy of his book *The Spiritual Perspective: Key Issues and Themes Interpreted from the Standpoint of Spiritual Consciousness*:[7] "To Andrea, Don't ever forget your Ph.D., to unfold, to actualize your highest potential in *this life.*"

Also, de Coppens genuinely liked and enjoyed people, but this always appeared true insofar as they gave him an audience for his ideas. He wrote and lectured a great deal about groups, and with a degree in sociology that is not surprising. I had the impression that he loved, and wanted to be loved for, his ideas, rather than his actions. Peter was someone who wanted to be looked up to, admired, important, loved. This is not to say he was purely an intellectual; no, he

---

[7]Peter Roche de Coppens, *The Spiritual Perspective: Key Issues and Themes Interpreted from the Standpoint of Spiritual Consciousness* (Washington, D.C.: University Press of America, 1980).

was active and enjoyed sports in his youth (skiing, like a true Gemini). But he never appeared to be the kind of person who would consider getting his hands dirty in a workshop or garden. I may, however, be wrong here, as he participated in charitable relief for the nation of the Ivory Coast, although the details of what occurred are not known to me.

Peter's coming of age was at the height of liberal social idealism and its stepchild, the New Age Movement, wherein it was believed that ideas would change the world and bring us all to enlightenment. The naive idealism of the Alice Bailey brand of Theosophy and its insidious influence on nearly every spiritual and psychological school of the mid-twentieth century appears to have had a large influence on his views. However, in the end, these grand ideas did not change, nor could they have changed, anything on a global scale, as good ideas are not enough. Now, a quarter-century later, we are seeing that the path to hell is paved with good intentions, especially when they are not backed up by real, deep-seated wisdom, compassion, and strength.

This is a critical point for me, in that it places de Coppens in the role of *teacher*, but not that of a *leader*, as a man squarely in the psychological and spiritual mindset of his time. I am not sure if he simultaneously held two contradictory views, but it appears that he may have: one of personal elitism and one of collective enlightenment. However, he did speak of the usual "cleansing" of the earth so common in those days (and even now), after which there would be a utopian world run by the spiritual elite. Maybe he truly believed, as did Alice Bailey, that the United Nations would be the vehicle for such transformation. Regardless, he was taking no chances and made it clear that Montreal was to be his retreat should things turn badly in the United States on this worldwide march toward utopia. Like his predecessors, the term "psycho-spiritual" is used extensively throughout his writings to demonstrate the blending of psychological and spiritual ideas and practices.

Now, it would be very easy to get hung up on de Coppens's personality, just as it would on Lisiewski's, and repeat the mantra of the German adept—"human, all too human"—when reflecting about my relationship to him, but that would be missing the forest for the trees.

Despite this criticism of de Coppens, it is important to note that one of the most significant mystical, or meditative, experiences of my life occurred working with one of the methods described in his book, *The Invisible Temple*. It had to do with discovering a powerful and inspirational archetype to guide you, the Divine Ideal, and is derived from the writings of Roberto Assagioli, the founder of Psychosynthesis.

To Peter I owe my interest and in, and subsequent study of, Psychosynthesis—he stated that Assagioli had told him his greatest disappointment was his own students. Later, as part of my research for my Master's Project in Counseling at Rhode Island College in 1989, I would realize what this meant, with the various organizational crises that would strike to the heart of the Psychosynthesis movement in the 1970s. I received an "A+" on the paper, and my written adviser comments stated, "An impressive paper!!! I like your willingness to select something 'different' for presentation and something complex and esoteric...well done!!!! Good!!!! [signed] Vin [Dr. Vincent Calia]."

During one of my visits with Peter, over Andrea's spring break from her graduate studies at Brown University, we returned home to visit with friends and relatives, and one Sunday morning I made the ninety-minute drive to visit him. We spoke about lecture topics, and the importance of being published, so as to be a "known quantity" someone recognized, rather than simply a local speaker. To be published was "to be." I can personally attest to the truth and power behind that statement; that is among the best advice I have ever been given. When I published my first article, "Pow-Wow, Psalms, and German Magical Folklore" in the Samhain 1993 issue of *Mezlim*, suddenly what I had to say had some weight to it. I was published in a respectable esoteric journal with some scholarly as well as practical value. This would only increase over time with each additional article I would publish. Later I would be able to send him a copy of my first book, *The Path of Alchemy*,[8] to demonstrate that I had taken the teaching to heart. Andrea would we even ask on occasion, "Did you send Peter a copy of your book?" Yes, dear, I did.

While I never saw him pick up a dinner check, he did establish a scholarship fund at the university in honor of his mother. Adhering to the traditional European perspective that teaching esoteric spirituality was an "avocation, not a vocation," he was ever active in that domain. Even after retirement, Peter organized a public program on spirituality and wellness at East Stroudsburg University (ESU), and hosted a local television program along the same lines. Always the focus of attention, the center of activity—a whirlwind, in fact, with his signature beret, pipe, and kiss on both cheeks. Ever the teacher, the performer, bringing people together with ideas—he was a true Gemini, and if he did not have Leo rising, he should have!

On the announcement for the seminar series he was running at ESU in 2010-2011 it states: "There are three essential attributes that human beings have always and will always seek, both unconsciously and consciously. These are knowledge to provide meaning and understanding, love to provide motivation and appreciation, and will to provide energy and power. These are truly fundamental to express ourselves and create both our becoming and our world. In this series we will direct our attention and analysis to knowledge."

"We will direct our attention to the analysis of knowledge"; words well spoken by a lover of ideas, of humanity, and of love itself, and the Great Work still to be done. Thank you, Peter, for your ideas and the impact they have had on my life.

---

[8]Mark Stavish, *The Path of Alchemy: Energetic Healing and the World of Natural Magic* (Woodbury, MN: Llewellyn, 2006).

Over the last year or so I have been receiving communications
from individuals and publishers wishing to get into contact
with Dr. Joseph C. Lisiewski,[1] author of the now-famous
book *Ceremonial Magic & the Power of Evocation.*[2] When
Ceremonial Magic hit the occult scene in 2004 it caused
quite a stir, as its fundamental working principle hinged on
not changing the words or instructions given in traditional
grimoires or magical books—to work them *exactly* as given.
For many who had grown accustomed to the New Age notion
that ritual magic was something you could modify to suit
your needs at the moment, or even make up as you went
along, this was a horrifyingly rigid and orthodox statement.
To make matters worse, Dr. Lisiewski also stated that to
modify the rituals in any form risked both failure in the rite
as well as a tremendous psychic and physical backlash from
trying to shortcut the instructions (or "hot wire" it, if you
will) for personal convenience. Lisiewski's writing style was

---

[1]The tense of this article as originally published is herein maintained.
For a fuller presentation, see the memoir by Mark Stavish, *The Magical
World of Dr. Joseph Lisiewski* (IHS Publications, 2017).

[2]Originally published by New Falcon Press (2004) and currently
available through The Original Falcon Press.

129

equally parts of Paracelsian "caustic bombastic thrashings" and clear instruction on how things are to be done, with emphasis on getting the desired material results.

It is here, emphasizing the results—material results at that—wherein Lisiewski stood out from among many who would claim to be his peers in the field of ceremonial magic. You see, Lisiewski had a unique pedigree: he was one of a few people fortunate enough to have studied all seven years of alchemy with Frater Albertus at the Paracelsus Research Society (later renamed Paracelsus College) and for fourteen years was a close friend of Dr. Israel Regardie. The relationship between Lisiewski, Albertus, and Regardie is detailed in *Israel Regardie and the Philosopher's Stone: The Alchemical Arts Brought Down to Earth.*[3]

In his inscription to the signed copy he sent me, Lisiewski wrote the following:

> Feb. 4, 2009
>
> To my very dear friend and collaborator in these things, Mark Stavish. Thanks so much for the Introduction to this book, and for your encouragement in writing it. For if the truth be known, if it were not for you, it would have never been penned. Have a good (2nd) read!
>
> Joseph C. Lisiewski, PhD.
>
> (Joe)

Our final work together would be *Howlings from the Pit: A Practical Handbook of Ceremonial Magic, Goetia & Theurgy,*[4] which was a compilation of articles from his highly successful

---

[3] Joseph C. Lisiewski, Ph.D., (introduction by Mark Stavish), *Israel Regardie and the Philosopher's Stone: The Alchemical Arts Brought Down to Earth* (Tempe, AZ: The Original Falcon Press, 2008).

[4] Joseph C. Lisiewski, Ph.D., (introduction & commentary by Mark Stavish), *Howlings from the Pit: A Practical Handbook of Ceremonial Magic, Goetia & Theurgy* (Tempe, AZ: The Original Falcon Press, 2011).

and profitable electronic newsletter of the same name. Dr. Lisiewski hired me to compile, edit, and add commentary to the material so that it would be more organized than it was in its original magazine-style format. He stated that given the length, duration, and nature of our relationship, I was the only one he knew and trusted sufficiently to undertake this task of taking his, at times, difficult writing style and clarifying the ideas for a new and different audience—one not necessarily grounded in ceremonial magic or historical grimoire work. In addition to his generous payment for my work, an amount that would take a while to be returned on standard book commissions, I was also given complete rights to this particular title by Dr. Lisiewski. *Howlings* was published by The Original Falcon Press in April 2011.

For those unfamiliar with the occult publishing world, New Falcon Press was established by Dr. Alan Ronald Miller (12 July 1943 - 9 February 2008), better known as "Dr. Christopher Hyatt," and Nick Tharcher "around 1980." In late February 2008, Miller's widow Linda Miller and surviving business partner Nick Tharcher founded The Original Falcon Press after, as their website states, "unsavory events" unfolded following Hyatt's death. These unsavory events (as I understand them) involve Alan's son having his father's will changed shortly before the older Miller's death to have the business put in his name.

As Lisiewski's close friend, co-worker, confidant, and here even semi-official biographer, our first conversation started late on a Sunday night, around 9:00 PM, and lasted for over two hours (I think closer to three). He called me weekly and eventually daily for over five years, and several times a week after that. His calls arrived like clockwork in the late afternoon, as Joe's schedule is to work across the night and into the early morning. I had the privilege of casting his natal chart (April 16, 1949; Ashland, Pennsylvania, 10:55 AM; Joseph Charles Lisiewski; Confirmation Name: Anthony), to which he compared the reading Israel Regardie had done for

him using the traditional Golden Dawn system of astrology.
I hear all of his rants and ravings about a life spent—and at
times wasted—in magic and alchemy, and understood more
deeply, clearly, and precisely than anyone how he came to
be the person he was, along with the important message he
had to tell—no, *scream*—to those entering the occult path.
It is no surprise that there are many wonderful similarities in
the personalities, temperament, and practical skill sets of Dr.
Lisiewski and William Gray, a man described as "reeking of
psychism like he reeked of incense." Gray was a formidable
magician capable of very definite manifestations in this world.
The same is true of Dr. Lisiewski. His magic was and is about
power; his mysticism was and is about divine union as the
way to that power. That was a hard lesson to learn, for him,
as well as for many current struggling magicians. "In the end,
they all become mystics," is a favorite quote of Lisiewski's.

While our official meeting occurred in May 2005, we had in
fact exchanged several emails in the late 1990s. Unfortunately—
and I can remember it so clearly—my computer crashed, and
I was left without means of contacting him. Lisiewski had
emailed me informing me of his relationship to Albertus and
Regardie, and told me that he resided in Pennsylvania. He
extended an invitation to open correspondence. Later, when
I came across *Ceremonial Magic*, I remembered his emails, or
rather occult pedigree, and asked several of my old Philosophers of Nature associates, who were also PRS alumni, if
they knew of Joseph Lisiewski. Jack Glass, the only person
to attend all seven years of PRS training twice, confirmed
the name, his work, and his stated relationships. Similar con-
firmations were given by others, and Pat Zalewski suggested
in an email that I might find alchemical discussions with
Lisiewski of value.

Oddly, life, like magic, is rarely linear. Just as my contact
with Lisiewski was delayed about six years, it was also after
my initial contact with Lisiewski in the the late 1990s that I
received an email from a Roman Catholic priest (who was an

active-duty chaplain in the U. S. Army) asking for assistance in preparing for the Abramelin operation. I prepared some guidelines for him; in addition, we met one evening at the temple of The Wyoming Valley Society for Esoteric Studies, located on the third floor at 239 Schuyler Avenue, Kingston, Pennsylvania, to discuss his proposed work. During this time he briefly mentioned some work that he did earlier in his youth with a friend. Years later I would find out that the man standing before me was in fact Lisiewski's assistant in his very first evocation as outlined in *Ceremonial Magic.* I spoke once more with the chaplain, this time around 2008-2010, and the events as given by Lisiewski were confirmed to me. All hell had broken loose, and it played no small role in his career choice.

Despite having withdrawn from the public scene, Lisiewski is still a controversial figure in the magical world—although less so than when he was doing his regular publishing.

In late winter or early spring of 2011 I went to Shamokin, Pennsylvania, to visit a building owned by a good friend of mine. We had known each other in college and he was a guest at my wedding, but it was not until hearing from him nearly twenty years later as Worshipful Master of one of the most prestigious Masonic Lodges in the area that we got to go from being acquaintances to friends. The building is a beautiful example of late-nineteenth/early twentieth century coal-country wealth. With a retail store and offices on the first floor, the second, third, and fourth floors were home to the Masonic lodge, and constituted a men's club that at one time would have included the business and political elite of the region. Walking through the building was like walking back in time, as we examined several rooms that had seen little use in years. On one of the playing card tables there was a newspaper laid out as if it had just been put down while its reader went to the nearby 7-Up bottle vending machine to get a drink. The date was from the late 1970s. This was, and still is, a beautiful building carefully being restored, and is a jewel for the town. When I mentioned my visit to Lisiewski, he immediately began to describe the unique interior of the retail space, as this had been one of his favorite haunts as a young boy. It also appears in one of his novels which takes place in a fictitious town in the Pennsylvania coal regions.

Hans Nintzel and Curt Coblarz are well known in the American alchemical community and were former classmates of Lisiewski's at PRS. Our discussions would often come back to these two men, as I had known them both, but not to the same level of intimacy as had Lisiewski. Nintzel was a pivotal figure in the twentieth-century English-speaking alchemical movement. The RAMS, or Rare Alchemical Manuscript Series, books which he published for decades, were—and for many still are—the working alchemical texts used in much practical laboratory work. At great cost to himself and his family, Nintzel obtained rare manuscripts, had them translated into English, and made them available in photocopy form. According to Lisiewski, Hans spent a great deal of his time at PRS in the library, leaving the practical lab work and reports to Lisiewski. Several other people have mentioned to me that although Nintzel taught practical laboratory alchemy, he was more of a bookworm than a lab rat.

I spent some time with Hans at various PON conferences and found him to be a likable and sincere fellow, if not at times a bit abrasive (more by accident than design). I am told that Jean Dubuis held Nintzel in a very special place in his heart for all of the work that he did to develop alchemy in the United States. I spent a weekend with Hans and a dozen or so of his close students at his house near Dallas, Texas, 13-16 January 1995. His wife Jody was warm, kind, and a wonderful hostess to all of us sleeping on the floor, couch, and various spaces around her home. Hans spoke of his time at PRS, his relationship with Regardie, and initiation into a Hermetic order in Los Angeles. The experiences I had during the visit were very profound and remain with me to this day, including the fortuitous arrival of a Horsetail plant stone, made for Hans by a French alchemist. I was given a thin sliver from its black taffy-like strip to try. On the back of the door to Hans's study was a wonderful poster which I hope to find a copy of some day. It illustrated a magician in ceremonial robes looking up at a huge demonic being; the text below read the famous line from *The Case of Charles Dexter Ward* by H.P. Lovecraft: "Do not call up that which you cannot put back down." Good words of advice for any novice magician.

I later wrote and published an article entitled, "A Weekend With Hans: Alchemy the Old-Fashioned Way."[5] Several years ago one of Hans's sons sent me an email thanking me for the kind article in memory of his father's contributions.

While I cannot say for certain, I must think that the work of Hans and others has weighed heavily on the formation of Lisiewski's attitude toward practical occult work—with emphasis on the word *practical*. At one point I sent Lisiewski a three-inch white three-ring binder containing a copy of various notes and instructions that Nintzel had compiled from his time at PRS and thereafter. It included a travel diary of his journey to France (an alchemical pilgrimage, if you will), along with additional notes of experiences he had with various practitioners of the Art. The material was given to me by Russ House, and given Lisiewski's relationship to Hans and Albertus I wanted his opinion on the laboratory material it contained.

However, it is the reality that Hans devoted his life to alchemy, as have so many others that Lisiewski and I know. Many are dead. They have not achieved the Philosopher's Stone, nor from their lives anything close to it. They have suffered tremendous indignities at the hands of family, friends, enemies, and—worst of all—fellow Companions in the Art of Hermes. The speed with which the RAMS material was quickly scanned and dumped on the Internet—with pirated

---

[5]Reprinted in Appendix B of Mark Stavish, *The Magical World of Dr. Joseph Lisiewski* (IHS Publications, 2017).

copies of CDs containing the various volumes being sold by people who had nothing to do with its compilation, translation, transcription, and formatting for publication back when everything had to be done by hand or with a typewriter—is staggering. It, like so many routine thefts that happen within the "spiritual community," is a condemnation that speaks louder than any squeaky "blessed be" or "namaste." It is this disregard for the hard work of others, and disrespect for their sacrifices, that truly irritated Lisiewski.

Few people know this—I am very sure that I am not breaking a confidence when I mention that Lisiewski took out a FHH loan to be able to afford his alchemical studies at PRS. His life, when not working at Paulsen Wire and Rope (Sunbury, PA) as an engineer, was dedicated to alchemy and magic. His wife tolerated—as do so many (my own included)—the various eccentricities that go with those for whom the Great Work has become an obsession. This would be later widened to open room for his graduate academic work in mathematics and physics, but essentially, the focus would be the same: The Great Work.

It was his "all or nothing" approach to occultism that made Lisiewski the single person Regardie would recall as being second only to Crowley. Total commitment is what is required on the Path. Students are told this often; however, few actually grasp the meaning or undertake the commitment. He was totally dedicated to his teachers—thus opening himself up to a certain degree of manipulation by them, as he would find out Albertus could be very compartmentalized in his dealings with people. Lisiewski built a furnace as a challenge from Albertus. This furnace eventually came into the possession of Art Kunkin who, when I spoke to him about it, was unaware of who had created it. I first met Art Kunkin at the Philosophers of Nature alchemy conference held at the Wild Rose (Girl Scout) Camp Ground in September 1994. An article summarizing this event (entitled "Pass the Sulphur, Salt, and Mercury If You Please") appeared in *Gnosis*

Magazine. It was the first article of mine to appear in *Gnosis.* It was also at this seminar that Kunkin gave me a copy of an interview with him that appeared earlier in *Gnosis,* complete with an errata sheet he had compiled.[6]

Curt Coblarz-Schmidt was also at this conference, and to my knowledge had attended all of them. He was a thin, wiry fellow. His upbringing was hard, the eldest of a large family of children whom he apparently was responsible for. Curt slept little and gave very technical presentations on various aspects of alchemy, often interspicing them with electronics. He was a talented electrical engineer, although it is not clear if he received any formal training. He was married at least once and divorced with no children. He ran afoul of the law on several occasions for his production of LSD—he claimed that pure LSD was not harmful, that it was the impurities that were dangerous—and before he lost contact with those closest to him he fell on hard times.

Curt told several stories that were hilarious in their own right, and even better when he told them in his matter-of-fact style. One involved having created an Orgone Energy Accumulator (after the writings of Dr. Wilhelm Reich) and mistakenly placing it on top of his Enochian Tablet of Water. He claimed that he had water problems all over his house for days until he realized what he had done. Another story involved his Chinese tutor, an older woman who did not look her age. Curt stated that she would sexually vampirize willing young men, who would be found passed out around her house at different times.

Joe had a terrible fondness for Curt and tried to get him employment in Pennsylvania. Curt would have none of it, saying he did not like the cold and preferred the warmth of Southern California. As of 2010-2011, Joe believed that Curt was dead, as all efforts to locate him had failed.

---

[6]Instructions for a furnace similar to the one Lisiewski built can be found in the booklet *Li'l Bertha: A Compact Electric Resistance Shop Furnace* by David J. Gingery (Bradley, IL: Lindsay Publications, 1984).

Having come of age in the declining coal regions of eastern Pennsylvania, it would come of no surprise to say that Lisiewski was a "self-made man." That is, despite tremendous personal obstacles, he went to college, majored in a demanding field, obtained a B.S. in Electrical Engineering, and later went on to get a Ph.D. in physics and mathematics. When I first met him he had recently returned to his hometown for a period of time. During our late-night conversations he would make mention of what it was like growing up there as a child and how it had changed—something I can relate to, having seen similar changes in the area where I was born and came of age. Occasionally our conversations would be interrupted by children who came asking for money, soda, or simply to talk. Apparently the street urchins had taken a liking to him, and he to them. His generosity is not well known, and he likes to keep it that way, believing that charity is best done in silence. I know that he has sent a considerable amount of books, printed materials, and CDs to his students and friends alike. If he liked it—and he could be a very hard man to please—he wanted to share it with those he cared about.

While Regardie and Albertus played the major roles in shaping Lisiewski's occult life among the "Masters of the Art" long gone, it was Éliphas Lévi and A. E. Waite that he liked the most. Lévi because—despite his questionable reputation as both a historian and a practicing magician— he had managed to obtain a comfortable and respectable position for himself and was "without want" (a good place to be in life). He admired Waite for much the same reasons I do. Waite came from a poor background and struggled against the arrogance of wealthy snobs like Crowley; while he had little in the way of formal education, he managed to carve out a name and place for himself in history. Waite knew what it was like to have dirt under his nails. He was someone both Lisiewski and I could relate to.

During our conversations I was given insight into the darker areas of occult practice, and by this I do not mean simply demonic evocation, but the stranger and more troubling areas of the human psyche and the cosmos. The psychic world is close to ours, closer than most would like to admit, and once the veil is pierced, a host of invited and uninvited guests can come through. One of the more intriguing areas of magic written about by Lisiewski in his newsletter (and later detailed in his book of the same name) *Howlings from the Pit* is the ritual of "The Watcher." The practice as outlined is extremely precise in the equipment needed—however, this is part of the defense against someone simply working the ritual and getting success. You see, the ritual (like nearly all of Solomonic magic) is difficult, and it is in the difficulty and successful carrying out of the ritual's specific requirements that the energy for success is derived. I have seen similar ritual practices and performed them myself, with similar results—all equally frightening when the unseen hand or presence is felt. But it is the ability to maintain one's composure at the critical moment that gives one mastery, not simply sensing the invisible presence. The words of Lovecraft echo in my ears: "Do not call up that which you can not put down"—good words to place above the portal to one's temple, just as "Patience" is a good word to put above the portal to one's laboratory.

In addition to having written numerous books on magic and the occult, Lisiewski also wrote several novels. His book *The Altar Path* was a veiled magical reflection on his childhood in Kulpmont, Pennsylvania,[7] and his other novel *Nightshadow* looked at his research while in the United Kingdom (Wales) during his thesis defense.[8] Here, he believes that the true nature of necromancy is not to raise the dead, but to be raised *from* the dead. He stated to me several times that he spent a considerable amount of money advertising his books

---

[7] Joseph C. Lisiewski, *The Altar Path* (Bloomington, IN: Author-House, 2007).

[8] Joseph C. Lisiewski, *Nightshadow* (Bloomington, IN: AuthorHouse, 2007).

in national newspapers, but that it did not pan out. After considerable research he finally opted for Author House as the Print-On-Demand printer for his books. It is no surprise that he eventually became upset with the way they were treating him—stating that his royalty checks did not match sales (having done some checking)—and believed he was being stolen from. He considered purchasing his own P.O.D. equipment for $250,000 but decided against it. He spent a considerable amount of time discussing this project with me and the owners of Health Research Publishing, who offered their technical assistance in understanding the business side of operations. His electronic PDF newsletter *Howlings from the Pit* (a name which I gave it, along with the name for the book) was extremely profitable for him.

During one of our discussions regarding meditations on The Cube, a symbol commonly applied to Malkuth in Kabbalah (and sometimes to Yesod) (described in detail in the *Sepher Yetzirah* as "The Cube of Space"), we noticed a peculiar phenomena. This was the appearance of a door and sense of the presence of other intelligences. Lisiewski felt that these beings were guardians of some sort—I called them "Archons" out of habit—and that this door was a trap one should never go through. I am uncertain of that point. It is unclear if this phenomena has been written about by others, as neither of us has seen it anywhere.

If I am asked what it is that I learned from my relationship with Dr. Joseph Lisiewski, it is this:

ONLY THE RESULTS MATTER.

This is a hard lesson. It is neither warm nor comforting; it offers little hope and much recrimination. Failure is seen for what it is: personal and painful. Success is hard earned, and not to be treated lightly. Such an understanding can make one hard if they let it. Yet the Path in part is designed to *make* us hard, hard so that we can support the weight of the cosmos on our shoulders, so that we can not only soar like the Eagle, but have the strength of the Bull as well. This is no different from what I have been told in nicer and more eloquent ways by Tibetan lamas and yogis. Yet, when Lisiewski says it, it is hard-edged. The bloodshed of decades of experience was always seeping though.

In addition, there were other lessons learned, some a little more palatable to the weak-hearted and gentle folk of modern spirituality, but nonetheless critically important once the above truth is branded into one's consciousness.

1. There is objective and subjective. The objective reflects the subjective and is to serve it. The subjective is the world of causes, and the objective is the world of effects.
2. If we cannot get the objective world to reflect our subjective desires and aspirations, then all occult practices are worthless from a practical point of view.
3. Magic and Mysticism are not the same, nor do they share the same goals.
4. Mysticism can be more powerful than magic, when the powers of the mind are applied directly without the intermediary of symbols and ritual.
5. If magic and mysticism have no practical value, then life is just a bloody battle for survival.

This may sound somewhat materialistic, but it is important to remember that the Hermetic axiom is, "As above, so below; as below, so above...to accomplish the work of the One Thing." The material world is as divine and spiritual as the mental and psychic worlds for, in fact, *there is no difference between them.*

It is this failure to consistently get the desired results from magical and various occult practices that pushed Lisiewski to re-evaluate his work in the Golden Dawn system, from which he came to the well-known conclusion that "the Golden Dawn is an eclectically imbalanced system." In short, it is top-heavy. Too much is piled on—Hebrew, Egyptian, Enochian, Christian—all hoping that if you throw enough against the wall, *something* has got to stick or, in this instance, *work*—work being defined as getting the desired results, not just "changes in consciousness at will," but in the environment, in one's day-to-day life.

These changes were not only experienced by Lisiewski, but according to him, by his wife as well, who on several occasions begged him to stop certain operations. He stated that during one operation, a dark figure of a man was continually appearing on the edge of the property of their rented townhouse. Another time he went to obtain his "dagger with the black handle"—a tool of Solomonic magic used only in rites of death and destruction, which Lisiewski claimed demons feared only second to the so-called "Blasting Rod" described in detail in his publication *Howlings from the Pit*—when his wife noticed a trail of blood coming from his hand. Lisiewski stated that he did not notice cutting himself, but that the dagger wanted "to drink." A similar remark was made by H. H. Shenphen Rinpoche regarding "the demon of the weapon" that encourages us to act violently when we own weapons, and the reason why Tibetan practices are heavy on purification and offerings. It was also during the "death of the homunculus" that Lisiewski felt the most regret and suffering for having undertaken the operation.

Several times during our regular chats, Lisiewski had mentioned that he was surprised that we had remained friends for as long as we had. While he had made many friends over the years, after two or three years they would part, and not always on the best of terms. Lisiewski has a fantastic memory, in part (he said) from a magical operation he performed decades ago. He can repeat conversations almost word for word, and while not always correct in reasoning and conclusions, he is correct often enough to easily turn a simple discussion into a debate, and from that, into an argument.

So, how is it that we got along so well for such a good run? Very simple, I told him: I accept you for who you are. I did not ask him or expect him to be anything or anyone else. He is a trained physicist. By nature this is an intellectually demanding field, and egos are made and destroyed in very heated arguments. I simply accepted that as his strength, not a weakness. While some of it definitely rubbed off on me, I do hope that some of my patience rubbed off on him. Having someone who looks at the operations of the mind, occult theory, and magical rites with the clarity of a scientist looking for causes and effects for consistent repeatability is exceedingly rare—too rare. The ability to have alchemical samples analyzed in a few days' time for nothing more than the cost of postage was well worth listening to the amusing profanity-laced tirades about publishers, authors, or the occasional political candidate.

This inability to accept our teachers for who they are rather than how they stack up against our laundry list of expectations of what they *should* be like is a major cause for the often violent and damaging rifts between students and teachers, just as it is among friends. This does not mean that we should accept abusive and possibly harmful behavior from our teachers or friends when it involves us, only that we have to always be clear about what it is we are in the relationship for, and what it is we are getting out of it as well as bringing to it. This level of self-reflection is rare but *critical* if we are to truly learn from anyone, let alone a would-be guide on the Path of Return. Not all guides can take us to the end of the journey, but many guides properly chosen—and properly left—can take us step-by-step along the Way.

When I say my daily prayers, and ask that all beings of the Three Worlds be freed from ignorance and suffering, just as Jesus had done when he entered into Hell to preach to the damned, and when I include prayers of gratitude to each of my spiritual teachers, as well as companions, I include Lisiewski as all three: teacher, companion, and friend.

JEAN DUBUIS

(29 APRIL 1919 - 6 APRIL 2010)

TOUCHING ETERNITY

19 April 2010

The following article was first published on 19 April 2010, and is being republished here in memory of the passing of Jean Dubuis, one of the twentieth century's foremost advocates of practical laboratory alchemy.[1]

In light of the recent announcement regarding the death of Jean Dubuis, I have been asked by many how it is that he most deeply affected me and my spiritual path—in short, my unfoldment as a person. This is a difficult question to answer because the effect was a complex one, subtle and yet direct, often taking time to rise to the level of my being consciously aware of it. This is not unique when dealing with a good guide in these matters, but a common occurrence that is experienced personally, and therefore intimate often beyond words. However, on an intellectual level (the starting point of much of this work) the most noticeable area of Jean's influence is in my assertion that there is only one set of laws for the universe and that they affect the material and spiritual in the same manner—if not, there would be chaos. Or as the

---

[1]For more information on Jean Dubuis, see the interview conducted with him by Mark Stavish on the Institute for Hermetic Studies website. See also Chapter 49 of Peter Marshall, *The Philosopher's Stone: A Quest for the Secrets of Alchemy* (London: Pan Books, 2002).

Emerald Tablet states, "As above, so below; as below, so above. To accomplish the Work of the One Thing."

I would even go so far as to say there is only one law in the universe: Karma, or Cause and Effect. Everything is Cause and Effect, and that is that. There is nothing special about this principle; however, in the West it has taken on moralistic tones. Jean referred to karma as Universal Justice, although he clearly stated that karma is not the Law of the Talon but rather a pressure that keeps us moving forward when we would rather sleep—it is what aids us in our Becoming. This is in total harmony with the teachings of the Ancient or Original Translation School of Tibetan Buddhism (Nyingma); two of its leading luminaries, Khenchen Paldren Sherab and Khempo Tsewang Dongyal stated at one of their annual Dzogchen Retreats that "karma is the activating of one's own self...everything is karma...everything has a cause, and cause has an effect...cause and effect are always consistent and connected." We need to heed this well, as it is the foundation stone of all that we do.

It is through my first encounter with Jean that I realized esoteric ideas could—and more importantly *must*—be stated in clear language. For too long I had become accustomed to the meaningless and empty droning of would-be adepti as they rambled on from one pseudo-kabbalistic or alchemical cliché to another, all the while acting as if what they were saying was crystal clear. Jean shattered this notion in a single stroke through his simple and direct explanations of the most complex areas of esotericism known. I remember well the first moment I heard him lecture at the Philosophers of Nature (LPN-PON) Conference held at the Wild Rose Conference Center near Wheaton, Illinois. I was unfamiliar with the material he was discussing on the Flamel Path, but it appeared from the apparatus and other materials that he had a clue about what he was talking about. Later, when he discussed the various mansions in Kabbalah, I realized in an instant that this man knew what he was discussing not from theory, but from experience. Later that year I attempted the "Contact with Eternity" method (called *Portæ Lucis*) and I remember in vivid and stunning detail the effects it had on me as I stood there one early morning in my apartment living room in East Providence, Rhode Island. All time had ceased to exist, and space crushed in on me as it, too, began to come to an end for me.

Of course it is as a result of the journal published by The Philosophers of Nature—*The Stone*—and my participation in the organization as the Director of Research for the ORA (Occult Research and Applications Project) that I was able to do my greatest and most significant writing on occult practices. I say "significant" because the material produced then continues to shape my writing to this day. I was told that Jean read everything that was produced in *The Stone*, and that he was pleased with my contributions.

On a more personal level, what I received most from being associated with Jean via PON and its truly selfless staff of volunteers, was the importance of learning to rely on myself for my growth, to learn from but not be dependent on outer teachers and guides, and to balance this independence with (as Jean would say) "not loving my ideas too much"—being open to what could be learned from others who (while they may not be perfect) can contribute to my advancement along the Path of Return. While clearly of a Western perspective on esoteric matters, Jean was fond of quoting Siddhartha, Lord Buddha, who said, "Do not believe because you saw the written word of an ancient sage; do not believe on the authority of masters or priests. But accept as truth and conform your life to what agrees with your experience and, after a profound study, satisfies your reason and leads to your good."

One saw this doctrine most strongly emphasized by Jean in some form in nearly every presentation he gave, even early on in his first set of lessons, *Fundamentals of Esotericism*, where he writes about egregores, or collective thought

forms created by various esoteric and initiatic organizations.[2]
Jean belonged to numerous esoteric orders in France and
knew many of the leaders of other groups, including those of
the notorious Solar Temple, whose members in Canada and
Switzerland committed suicide, sparking a flurry of anti-cult
activity across Europe in the 1990s.

Prior to establishing The Philosophers of Nature, Jean
resigned all of his affiliations, stating that one must be *free*
to be truly initiated in the interior path (of which alchemy
and Kabbalah were the principal tools), as the means and
methods used by many modern groups are ineffective and
the leaders of many of these groups are often well meaning
but incompetent, wasting time and energy arguing over the
authenticity of various lineages. Additionally, many are actually deceiving their members about the actual motives of the
organization's leaders, or are simply using the organization
as a source of revenue. The means of maintaining hold over
a large membership that does not always have direct contact
with other members or the leadership except through correspondence, according to Jean, was through the collective
mind, or *egregore*. For this reason, Jean encouraged those
who would pursue their Path to do so alone, or in small study
groups, but to avoid collective rituals. For this reason, The
Philosophers of Nature never held any collective rituals, and
on the one occasion I was asked to lead those attending a
conference in a Eucharistic practice, it was done within the
context of a lecture to avoid any suggestion of creating a
group mind.

I eventually resigned all of my affiliations as a result of this
(and other factors not relevant at the moment) in order to
test Jean's theory. While it took a while for the effects of the
collective mind to wear off, I eventually began to understand
what he was referring to and how the collective mind can

---

[2]For further information on the topic of egregores, see the forthcoming
book by Mark Stavish, *Egregores: The Occult Entities That Watch Over
Human Destiny* (Rochester, VT: Inner Traditions, 2018).

turn from being a guide in the beginning into a crutch, and eventually an obstacle in the end, if we are not careful and observant.

Oddly, it was Jean's insistence that he was "no guru" that led me to explore more deeply the role of teacher and student relationships in Western occultism. The old ways of mentorship are for the most part dead, and yet it is only through the "living word" that teachings come alive. This contact with a living, breathing example is essential for everyone at points along their journey. People impact other people in ways that a book, video, or correspondence course simply cannot. On closer examination, it was clear that what Jean meant by not being a guru was that he was not authoritarian in his teaching. Each person had to make what he taught their own, test it out, and see if it fit. He claimed no special authority based either on initiation, lineage, or secret teaching of any kind—only personal experience, which he freely shared as a possible guide for others. In fact, his whole focus was to assist people to learn methods that they could apply that would place them in contact with their Inner Master and thereby be free of the constraints of accidental or intentional error on the part of human guides.

A peculiar effect was that, as a result of Jean's utterly contagious confidence in the path he outlined and the tools he provided, I disposed of the greater part of my library on several occasions, pruning out material that was no longer directly supportive of my practice. As my practice became more focused and graduated, taking more time to go deeper into each step of the process, I discovered that the most important books I had were none other than my own notebooks, the record of my experiences, and that it was *there* that I would find both the questions and answers that would be the moving force on my Path. This was particularly true of Pathworking on the Tree of Life, and when I later directed others (over a multi-year period in the process), many stated that those were the most effective and deeply meaningful experiences they have ever had.

Many of us believe—and Jean may have even stated at some point—that in some respects it was getting more difficult to do alchemy than in the past. The costs involved, along with various health and safety laws in the last decade alone, have made it very difficult to perform mineral alchemy in contemporary urban settings. Mineral alchemy has always required copious amounts of time, talent, and treasure, and increasingly it seems that these are in short supply. Jean stated that esotericism was changing, as does everything, and he dedicated himself to perfecting a method of self-initiation that could be undertaken fairly easily by anyone, resulting in the *Portæ Lucis* method mentioned earlier, as well as in a series of machines that through visual, auditory, and magnetic stimulation to the brain could produce controlled and reliable out-of-body experiences. I had the opportunity to test-ride one of the earlier versions of these machines and can attest to their effectiveness. With Jean's passing, their future remains uncertain.

Jean touched many people with his healing abilities, expressed through alchemy as well as directly through the mind. This effect was further multiplied by the many people who benefited through making spagyric and alchemical tinctures of their own as a result of the lessons and articles he wrote, and sharing them with family and friends. One of the most powerful and simple tinctures to make was explained by Jean under a paper entitled "Alchemy Without a Laboratory," and detailed his experiences and method for making a tincture out of acorns that has some surprising power and wide-reaching healing capacity.

For me, the best way to remember Jean—particularly on a Sunday night when I have a tall glass of red wine before me— is through a poem he wrote. The following was translated by Patrice Maleze, Jean's close friend and companion in alchemical matters for many years and well known to those who attended PON conferences.

In reality
There is no god or devil,
No Jesus or Buddha
There is only each of us in only one Being in Unity.
You and me in Duality.
Tonight when I am you and me,
I know that I AM the Child of the Naught [Nothing-
ness],
When facing our Father, the Naught,
I will dominate him, I must to become the Infinite
Being of Eternity.
Nothing else is but a temporary, yet necessary Illu-
sion.

That thunder you hear just may be a wrestling match
going on in heaven.

When we look at our lives it is often easy to see who has made a significant impact on us, the choices we make, and the achievements we accomplish. For me, the principal person that would shape my life path was my great-uncle Edward Tischler.

The brother of my maternal grandmother, he was the second born of a family of seven children. His youngest sister Freda was my grandmother. Born on January 8, 1900, in or around Posen, in German-speaking Silesia, he emigrated with his parents and older brother Julius to the United States, landing at Ellis Island. While it was often thought by his sisters that he was "born on the ride over," a horoscope cast by him later in life shows Posen as his birth location.

The Tischlers made their way to Plymouth, Pennsylvania, where sponsors and a job in the mines awaited. It was the policy in those times that no one could enter the United States who did not have a sponsor, a job, and a clean bill of health upon landing.

Edward's father Augustus quickly left the mines and opened a small grocery store, and the family grew in size. At the age of seventeen, Edward—or Eddie as we called him— lied about his age, saying he was twenty-one to the Railroad

Board, and obtained a job on the Delaware and Lackawanna Railroad, at which he remained until retiring in 1965 as an engineer. Like many men of the time, he was handy with tools, and was an entrepreneur in the early radio industry, building them from scratch.

What makes Eddie unique is that while there was nothing particularly special about him in outward appearance, he was in fact a man deeply immersed in learning, self-improvement, and the mysticism of his forefathers. Born with a veil—a thin membrane of skin over his face—he was seen by the people of the time as someone born with the gift of spiritual vision, or clairvoyance. The land of Silesia was well known over several hundred years for its mystical orientation, with kabbalists, alchemists, and occultists of all kinds coming and going. His mother was illiterate in her native German, but had the ability to know things before they would happen. During the Influenza Epidemic of 1919, she would tend to the gravely sick with no fear for herself or her family. His father was also quite skilled in healing and other arcane practices.

It is no surprise that by the time Eddie was a young man he would become skilled in astrology, hypnosis, and even several forms of divination or fortune telling.

I remember when my brother's car was stolen. A few hours after hearing about it, Eddie said, "Don't worry. It will be returned in a few days." This was hard to believe, but within three days, the car had been found abandoned, no damage done (except for the charges to get it released from the Scranton police impound). I later discovered that Eddie had used the medieval practice of *geomancy*, related to astrology, to ascertain this prediction.

Another time he came over and announced that his brother-in-law had just died—he knew because he said that he saw him when walking up the steps, standing on the stairwell inside his house, wearing a brown suit and, of course, no shoes. His brother-in-law *was* buried in a brown suit, and the dead don't wear shoes. It was also related that he had saved his niece from certain death when she was gravely ill as a child—the doctor having filled out her death certificate except for the time.

When asked about these things, he would simply say—as the Bible tells us—"With God, all things are possible." Or if he was in the mood, he would give a longer explanation based upon the statement of Jesus: "These things which I do, so shall you, and even greater."

Among his greatness was his generosity, having faithfully supported the local Lutheran church, as well as the Red Cross, Salvation Army, the Silesian Brothers, and numerous other charities. When I went through his records after his death I found *annual* donations made during the depths of the Great Depression that would be the equivalent of over $1,500 in today's money—all from a railroader's salary plus a few radio repair jobs on the side. Additionally, during the Second World War, he and a group of like-minded mystics raised money to support a mysterious "Polish Princess" who was part of the resistance movement.

As a student of the mind, he could be found frequently in meditation and prayer, and would say, "All is suggestion. We are suggested into the world, and we are suggested out of it." For him, the power of belief reigned supreme. To this end, he had the quirky habit of routinely shutting off the sound to commercials when watching television. He would say, "It is all hypnotic suggestion."

My greatest memories are of taking him, when in his eighties, twice a month to meetings of the Wilkes-Barre Pronaos (Rosicrucian Order, AMORC), where as a member of the organization since 1927 he was treated with "elder statesmen" status. It was then that I got the chance to drive his 1954 Chevy, complete with chrome torpedo bumpers, bench seats the size of a sofa, and a steering wheel big enough to drive a truck with. I came to understand the meaning of the phrase "American engineering"!

In addition to AMORC he was associated with several New

Thought organizations during the 1920s and 1930s, as well as C. C. Zain's Brotherhood of Light, Martinist Order et Synarche, Traditional Martinist Order, and Dr. George Winslow Plummer's Societas Rosicruciana in America (SRIA).

His death came relatively quickly at the age of ninety-six. The Lutheran minister who presided over his funeral was at a loss for words when several of Eddie's fraternal brothers and sister appeared to pay their final respects, placing upon him the mystic symbol of the love and appreciation they had for him as their Elder Brother, that of a golden cross and a single red rose, upon which was inscribed the words of the seventeenth-century mystics: *Jesu Mihi Omnia* ("Jesus is my All").

The final words he said were: "We are hypnotized into this world, and we are hypnotized out of it. It is all by the power of suggestion. Guard your mind well."

With that, he closed his eyes.

Support from the Institute for Hermetic Studies

The Institute for Hermetic Studies is a non-profit organization offering a range of ongoing support to individual students and groups through online materials, seminars, and private tutorial. These include but are not limited to: basic, intermediate, and advanced instruction in the Hermetic Arts and Sciences, astrological consultations, assistance with psychic and spiritual crises, and training for ordination in the Minor and Major Orders of the Church of St. Cyprian the Mage of Antioch. All information regarding our programs is announced in our electronic newsletter VOXHERMES. For more information contact:

The Institute for Hermetic Studies
P.O. Box 4513
Wyoming, PA 18644-04513

www.hermeticinstitute.org
info@hermeticinstitute.org

Mark Stavish (Pennsylvania) is a respected authority in the study and practice of Western spiritual traditions. He is the author of numerous books, most recently the IHS Monograph Series, IHS Ritual Series, and the preceding volumes of IHS Study Guides, as well as *The Magical World of Dr. Joseph Lisiewski*, *The Path of Alchemy*, *Kabbalah for Health and Wellness*, and *Between the Gates: Lucid Dreaming, Astral Projection, and the Body of Light in Western Esotericism*. His works have been translated into nine languages worldwide. He is founder of both the Institute for Hermetic Studies (Wyoming, Pennsylvania), where he is Director of Studies, and the Louis Claude de St.-Martin Fund, a non-profit fund dedicated to the study and practice of esotericism.

Alfred DeStefano III (Virginia) is Editor and Publication Manager for the various Institute for Hermetic Studies titles, overseeing all aspects of interior book design. In addition to his occupation as a college instructor of mathematics, he has assisted in the production of numerous esoteric works, including the most recent Seventh Edition of Israel Regardie's *The Golden Dawn*, edited by John Michael Greer (Llewellyn).

Made in the USA
San Bernardino,
CA